CAPITALIZING

ON

KINDNESS

Why 21st Century Professionals Need to Be Nice

Kristin Tillquist

CAREER
PRESS

The Career Press, Inc.
Franklin Lakes, NJ

Copyright © 2009 by Kristin Tillquist

CAPITALIZING ON KINDNESS
EDITED BY KATE HENCHES
TYPESET BY MICHAEL FITZGIBBON
Cover design by Jeff Piasky
Printed in the U.S.A. by Book-mart Press

To order this title, please call toll-free 1-800-CAREER-1 (NJ and Canada: 201-848-0310) to order using VISA or MasterCard, or for further information on books from Career Press.

B CAREER PRESS

The Career Press, Inc., 3 Tice Road, PO Box 687,
Franklin Lakes, NJ 07417
www.careerpress.com

Library of Congress Cataloging-in-Publication Data
Tillquist, Kristin.
   Capitalizing on kindness : why 21st century professionals need to be nice / by Kristin Tillquist.
      p. cm.
      Includes index.
      ISBN 978-1-60163-038-4
   1. Business ethics. 2. Professional ethics. 3. Kindness. 4. Success in business. I. Title.

HF5387.T55 2009
650.1'3--dc22

                                                            2008032881

To my trinity:
my husband, John;
my mom, Pat; and
my friend, Ennette.

ACKNOWLEDGMENTS

I have many examples, successful "nice guys," in my life who are models of kindness and success. They deserve many thanks.

My first thanks are to my sweet husband, John, my love. I am lucky to have such a wonderful, unconditional booster, most loyal supporter and life partner. He is also a talented businessman and the best writer I know, and drafts of this book have greatly benefited from his review and editing.

My love and appreciation go to my mom, Pat, who was, appropriately, the very first person to read the book from start to finish. She is the epitome of the positive, likeable personality that so attracts others, and she is the most loving person I know.

Then, my dear friend, Ennette Morton, for her day-in-day-out support, insights, and extraordinary thoughtfulness. My colleague in politics, my coconspirator in fun, I am thankful for her daily presence in my life.

Next, my two mentors who are both friends and colleagues. Mayor Loveridge, the best boss there could be, unknowingly helped me formulate some of the philosophies expressed in this book…just by being who he is. And Jim Erickson, my encouragement buddy and sage advisor, who makes everyone he touches feel like a "winner."

And to Kristin Walder, my research assistant, who brought insights to this project that belie her youth.

Thanks go to The Career Press team who helped put it all together, including: Michael Pye, Laurie Kelly-Pye, Jeff Piasky, Kristen Parkes, Kirsten Dalley, Kate Henches, and Mike Fitzgibbon. Thanks also to my literary agent at Waterside Productions, Bill Gladstone, and to Ming Russell, for helping direct the book toward the business market.

There are lots of other people who have encouraged and helped in a myriad of ways and deserve my thanks. I would like to especially acknowledge:

Collette Lee, for her unbridled enthusiasm, and she and Gary for the use of their "writers retreat" in San Diego where the framework of this book was laid out.

Becky Whatley for giving me an incredibly inspiring book on writing, *Walking on Alligators: A Book of Meditations for Writers* (Harper San Fransisco, 1993), at exactly the right moment when inspiration was truly needed.

Members of the 951 Writers Club, including Chris Kearn, Michelle Oulette, Dulce Pena, Pattis Pettis Cotton, Teresa Rhyne, and Barbara Shackelton, who saw and commented on various parts of the book during our monthly gatherings. Special thanks to members Michelle Oulette and Barbara Shackelton for helpful comments and extensive editing, respectively.

Cathy Davies and Rowena Albanna for their excellent feedback on an earlier draft; their comments made a difference. And to Lynne Sihvonen, Ricki McManuis, my sister Shannon Graver, Rory Fiorito, Amro Albanna and Nousheen Huq for their help.

Family, friends, and colleagues…thank you for modeling the way of kindness.

CONTENTS

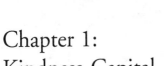

Chapter 1

KINDNESS CAPITAL

The more credit you give away, the more will come back to you. The more you help others, the more they will want to help you.

—Brian Tracy, author

The 21st century is not for the timid. It is not for the unprepared, unmotivated, or weak. To be successful in today's professional environment—characterized by technology, intense competition, global market forces, and escalating expectations—you need many things: determination, well-articulated goals, and a bit of luck. But, more than any of those, you need kindness.

The business world is a place for the vibrantly, positively, dynamically nice. Not the "roll over and play dead" of the passively nice. Not the "if I stay quiet and work hard, maybe I'll eventually get noticed" approach. Not the self-sacrificing, give-till-you-bleed kind of generosity. And not the "let everyone trample all over you" niceness. Rather, kindness becomes a business asset—*the* business asset—when you couple a caring attitude toward others with a strong and savvy business approach. Kindness not only helps others, it helps you be as successful as you want to be.

Often people see business as a choice between being kind and being successful. This is a fictitious trade-off. *Nice people are more successful.* They start with what is kind, and then (and only then), think of how benefits might flow to them. It is precisely *because* of our 21st-century business climate that the intentional development of kindness is so important. We can no longer conduct business as usual and expect to be successful. Yesterday's business style will not create today's business success.

Create Kindness Capital

More and more companies are recognizing the strategic value of social responsibility...

—Arthur A. Thompson Jr., business strategy author

This book will take you on a crash course in kindness and show you how to develop "kindness capital." Kindness capital is what is built up when you consciously set out to be kinder and to develop your skills at applying kindness. Kindness capital exists in the individual, in a company, and in society.

From those just starting their careers to the seasoned veteran, the benefits of developing kindness capital are immense. For use in all professional situations, decisions, and transactions, kindness makes the difference between tremendous success and "just getting by." Kindness, coupled with other professional skills and abilities, enables individual professionals to make their career goals and aspirations happen. Business owners—from mom-and-pop shops to corporate CEOs—have much to gain from kindness. What kind of benefits will you realize when you are kind? Will kindness *automatically* or *instantaneously* make you rich, successful, and well respected? No, not always, but it will set you on the course to having the things you want and being the person you want to be. When you learn to use kindness every day to achieve your loftiest goals and simplest everyday desires, you join the ranks of the most successful professionals and businesses on the planet. Just ask Oprah Winfrey, Colin Powell, Warren Buffett, and Sandra Bullock. Take a look at Google, L.L. Bean, and the Gap Inc. J.F.K and J.C. Penney knew it too.

Kindness capital results in increased productivity, reduced absenteeism, and a decreased likelihood of litigation. It makes it easier to attract and retain top-notch employees. It can make the difference between plodding along with a small market share and exploding into the market. Niceness will ensure you are a business of choice, a boss of choice, or an employee of choice.

Five powerful tools for developing kindness capital make such results possible:

1. The Power of Reputation: building a strong caring reputation.

2. The Power of Reciprocity: giving and garnering reciprocal kindnesses and favors from others.

3. The Power of Personality: learning to be someone that others like.

4. The Power of Thanks: being appreciative of
   others.

5. The Power of Connecting: connecting with
   others and building a strong network.

The Five Powers of Kindness are the complete package, a total solution, for professional success. Each of the Five Powers is largely a commonsense approach that you will readily recognize as a solid business choice. Kindness in business is at the core of what people *really* mean when they talk about "soft skills." Yet most people and businesses are completely unaware of how kindness affects business. Instead, they talk about customer service, communication skills, interpersonal abilities, and a myriad of other terms that point to simply demonstrating care for others in business.

Unfortunately, misunderstanding kindness in business makes for a lot of misguided efforts. Attempts at professional growth that neglect kindness offer only partial solutions. Communication skills without a firm grounding in kindness fall flat, leading to disingenuous and thin interactions. Leadership skills without a caring and genuine interest in those you lead will be transparent. The stellar education you use to impress others will only make weak allies without an interest in supporting you in times of need. In the following chapters, dedicated to each of the Powers, we will examine how to apply kindness to your career or business in order to achieve the best results for others, and for you. The "practice pointers" at the end of each chapter will help you implement the techniques you've learned.

Above all else, building kindness capital is about being self-aware, being conscious of your effect on others. We have a tremendous impact on each other throughout our personal and professional lives. Identify opportunities for kindness, and be more intentional about cultivating kindness capital in your professional life.

When you use the Five Powers, you raise the level of kindness capital all around you.

Go ahead and describe a valued coworker. What words would you use? What if you were to describe your ideal boss? Your favorite client? A stellar supplier or technology provider? Your best friend? How about yourself? Kindness is that highly desirable constellation of values and behaviors recognized as: respect, consideration, sincerity, forthrightness, helpfulness, understanding, patience, generosity, positiveness, caring, and just plain old everyday niceness.

These are the qualities that attract others, and win hearts, minds, loyalties…and business.

So, what does kindness look like at the corporate, rather than the individual, level? Can a company be nice? Who are the people to whom a company should be nice? In business, kindness has often been labeled "corporate social responsibility," but I think of it as "corporate kindness." Prime employees flock to "nice" companies, boosting their performance, quality, and customer loyalty. Starbucks practices corporate kindness through charitable giving, employee volunteer opportunities, and a positive work environment. Correspondingly, it attracts the best employees in the service industry and develops high customer loyalty—two conditions critical for a healthy bottom line. Google is another global company that has turned corporate kindness to its advantage—and into profits. Known for doing right in the communities in which it is based, and creating a welcoming environment for its employees, Google knows that niceness is, indeed, a business advantage. Neither Starbucks nor Google allows kindness to be seen as a weakness. Rather, they make niceness a key tool in their success, allowing them to garner market share, reap profits, and set themselves ahead of their competition.

However, few professionals or corporations currently boast kindness on their resume, in their professional biographies, in their advertising, or on their Websites. When asked for strengths or corporate values, few brag that kindness is their forte.

They should.

In a world full of choices, being nice is a smart business strategy. But there are barriers that get in the way of kindness if we let them. The good news is that most of these obstacles, the "kindness inhibitors," are indeed myths—mere figments of society's imagination. They fall by the wayside as we look at the facts and data that link kindness to success. A study initiated by Johnson & Johnson with the Ethics Resource Center in Washington, D.C., determined that businesses that adopt a written commitment to social responsibility, and act on that commitment, reap more profits than companies that don't.[1] Literally.

Johnson & Johnson's chairperson, James Burke observed: "If you had invested $30,000 in a composite of the Dow Jones 30 years ago, it would be worth $134,000 today. If you had put that $30,000 into these [socially and ethically responsible] firms—$2,000 into each of the 15 [in the study]—it would now be worth over $1 million.[2] Companies that make kindness part of their mission outperform those that don't.

More good news: The barriers are readily surmountable once we bust open the thinking that allows for their existence. I will show you how as we debunk one kindness inhibitor at the end of each chapter. As Henry Ford said, "Obstacles are those frightful things you see when you take your eyes off your goal." When you keep your eye on the goal of building kindness capital, these little barriers become insignificant and easily manageable.

But let me add an important caveat here: Niceness must be genuine to really work. Put-on kindness to garner favor, feigned interest to gain an advantage, or insincere compliments to mask an ulterior motive will quickly be seen through. Only when you cultivate a real interest in helping others succeed alongside you will you realize the full and lasting power of kindness. This book gives you a lens to not only learn the benefits of kindness as a business tool, but also to give you inspiration to cultivate and anticipate the best in, and for, others.

21st-Century Imperative

It's no use saying "We are doing our best." You have got to succeed in doing what is necessary.

—Sir Winston Churchill

What's more, 21st-century professionals can't afford *not* to be nice. Being mean, uncaring, or inconsiderate simply does not work. It is an unsuccessful approach to business, and it is increasingly unsuccessful as the 21st century rolls forward.

Kindness is needed more than ever during trying economic times. Old measures of success do not work anymore. The relentless, persistent, and creative application of kindness is a new market imperative and prerequisite to thriving in a challenging economy. Companies that fail to develop kindness capital are not as successful as their kind counterparts. Individual professionals who neglect the Five Powers cannot, especially in the long term, keep up with their peers, let alone their competitors.

Lack of kindness costs businesses, well, business. Often thought of as poor customer service, low kindness capital causes customers and clients to flee rapidly, and usually permanently. Particularly now, in the electronic age when there are so many choices, clients will simply move on if they suspect they are being treated poorly. They have many options. They will buy elsewhere, even at an elevated price, if they do not feel cared for.

Highly skilled employees are also highly sought after, and they will move on too—to companies that practice corporate kindness. Similarly, the stereotypical, cutthroat wheeler-dealer lasts only as long as his or her reputation holds out, which is not long at all. Once business partners learn that the wheeler-dealer doesn't have their best interests in mind, they won't do business with him again.

The successful 21st-century professional learns to work with others, not against them. Trying to force an outcome with a show of strength rarely works in business. At best, such bravado brings about one deal, one time. Rather, it is the more thoughtful search for mutual benefits that brings others around to the nice guys' way of thinking…and more business to their doorstep.

The Economy of Kindness

Human kindness has never weakened the stamina or softened the fiber of a free people. A nation does not have to be cruel to be tough.

—Franklin D. Roosevelt

Do good *and* do well. That is the business philosophy of the Southern California–based, active gaming company Actiga that so attracted my husband, John, and me that we became early investors in this then-risky high-tech startup. This simple guiding principle, coined by its president, Dale Hutchins, and expanded by CEO Amro Albanna, so impressed us that it overcame our usual fiscal conservatism. In conversation with Amro and his wife, Rowena, John and I explored the kindness approach to business. Amro explained that their style of success is founded on the idea that everything their company does should result in something good, something positive, for others. "When we focus on spreading good results, for customers, shareholders, and passers-by alike, we correspondingly do really well financially." This is the economy of kindness.

This "do good" business strategy is based in Actiga's main product line. Active gaming applications result in increased fitness and often a reduction in obesity for those who partake. In our increasingly sedentary society, Hutchins and Albanna believe that providing fun, family-based activity and entertainment is the right ticket, a wholesome approach that merges the ever-popular video game with physical fitness. Providing golf, tennis, snowboard, and exercise-cycle products is one way they feel they are doing good. But believing that kindness works in business, they also focus on conducting business in a way that benefits others…and themselves. Clearly they are on to something: their early 2008 public launch has confirmed fast growth and high shareholder value, vaulting the company to a valuation of more than $55 million at the time of this writing.

It is important to reconcile our philosophical approaches—about business, success, and values—to achieve maximum benefits for ourselves and others in the 21st century. To really embrace kindness as a business tool at the individual or corporate level, fundamental mindset shifts are required.

Soft Is Hard

First, we must shift from the hard-nosed approach to realizing that "soft is hard."[3] What might appear gentle, even cautious, can be a well-designed and highly effective business strategy. Robert McNamara, former U.S. Secretary of Defense and former World Bank president, captured the concept that caring about others in business is compatible with success when he said: "I don't believe there's a contradiction between a soft heart and a hard head." The so-called "soft skills" in business measurably impact all of the rest—ability to hire the best people, capability to secure financing, attracting and retaining a customer base, creating public acceptance, and, ultimately, achieving a strong bottom line.

Enlightened Self-Interest

The second shift is that there is not an inherent conflict between being self-interested and being kind. As a true optimist, I expect that people will do their best. I see countless examples each day in which people act kindly and help each other. People react to so many situations with honor and generosity in their personal and professional lives that they increase the collective kindness capital. But you do not have to be kind *only* because you feel kind and want to help others. Most people are motivated by both the value they can bring to others and their society *and* by the benefits that they can obtain for themselves. Former chairman of IBM Thomas J. Watson put it this way: "Our early emphasis on human relations was not motivated by altruism but by the simple belief that if we respected our people and helped them to respect themselves, the company would make the most profit." Think of this as *enlightened* self-interest.

But wait. Isn't there a contradiction here? How can you, for example, "take advantage" of the help of coworkers and still be kind to them? Is it wrong to curry favor with someone you know can put in a critical reference for the position you have been coveting for years? How can you make kindness your operating mantra in the workplace, while simultaneously capitalizing on the many advantages that others can accord you?

The writings of 18th-century philosopher Emmanuel Kant are especially valuable in making sense of our many symbiotic professional relationships. Kantian philosophy acknowledges that we all rely on other people as a means to an end, sometimes. However, he cautions that it is important to recognize the intrinsic value of others and not to treat them merely as a means to an end. Let's look more closely at this concept as it is fundamental to both building kindness capital and thriving in the 21st-century professional environment.

What is this "intrinsic value"? Intrinsic value is the recognition of fundamental worth and value that is independent of an outcome or result, independent of you and your desires. You and I would be hard-pressed, therefore, to say that there is intrinsic value in a chair. Its value comes from making a person who sits in it comfortable, so it serves as a means to an end, that of being comfortable. The value of the chair is understood only in relation to what it does for someone, so it cannot be said to have its own intrinsic value. Even if you had a particularly well-crafted and beautiful chair that you could call a piece of art, the chair's value would come from the aesthetic experience it creates for the person viewing it. The chair would not have its own value independent of the experience it provides a person.

However, people do have intrinsic value. Our worth is not dependent on how we act, what jobs we hold, what work output we create, or how we make others feel. Rather, our value is inherent in our very existence. If you agree with this basic philosophy (not so complicated really), then you must agree that each person you encounter is deserving of your kindness and respect.

With this mindset, you can simultaneously care about and respect others while at the same time enjoying and appreciating the ways in which they can benefit you. Enlightened self-interest is evident in many everyday scenarios—both personal and professional. In fact, most kind acts are performed for a variety of reasons that include, but are not limited to, the desire to be kind. Most corporate and individual giving—donations and sponsorships—result from a mixture of motivations. Certainly part of the reason is usually generosity and a desire to do good for others. Giving is often motivated by "baser" interests as well: getting the company's name out there, receiving thanks and recognition, and the chance to get something in return or to gain an advantage.

Unsurprisingly then, the lottery approach to fundraising is significantly more successful than regular fundraising. Lottery fundraising involves raising money in exchange for the chance to win a prize, such as tickets to a drawing or a new car. So the donor gets to give to whatever charity for which the lottery is raising money, and also has the chance to receive in a concrete sense.

Lottery fundraisers raise about 50 percent more dollars than regular fundraisers. The increased dollars result largely because many more people choose to donate (participation rates increase by roughly 100 percent) and because individual donors give more. This is enlightened self-interest in action: many more people will donate, and they will donate more, when they see the chance of direct benefits for themselves.[4]

Rather than feeling indignant or dismayed, think of the result: 50 percent more dollars are raised to go to the cause in need. This is a good outcome, no matter that the giving is not altogether altruistic in intent. Additionally, the charitable beneficiary's pool of future donors is greatly expanded—their mailing list is augmented with the new donor contact information. The mixed motivation brought about by the possibility of receiving a prize does not in *any way* diminish the value of those dollars. Everyone wins when you develop kindness capital.

Good Is Not Great

So far we have covered two mindset shifts: realizing that "soft is hard" and enlightened self-interest. The third major mindset shift that the practice of kindness in business requires is embracing the profound simplicity of the concept that *good* is not *great.* Or, rather, as best-selling leadership author Jim Collins coined the phrase: "good is the enemy of great."[5] The reason we are not as successful as we want to be is because we are good. Often we "self-handicap" and fail to strive for what we really want and can accomplish—sometimes out of fear, other times out of apathy.

Perhaps because you are doing pretty well in your professional career (you attracted a few new clients last year and no one is complaining about your performance), you feel that things are "good enough." And because you try to be fair to your colleagues and are (nearly) always polite, you feel that you are already "kind enough." If this approximates your current attitude, then you have not yet recognized the vast power of kindness capital in making your life everything you ever dreamed it could be. All of us can be kinder *and* more successful than we are now. The conscious development of kindness capital will move you from good to great. It takes only conscious thought and the Five Powers.

The Collateral of Kindness

Management is efficiency in climbing the ladder of success; leadership determines whether the ladder is leaning against the right wall.

—Stephen Covey

The collateral benefit of making these mindset shifts and spreading kindness is success. As you explore and implement kindness in your professional life, as you seek to move from good to great, you will want to take some time to determine what success really means to *you*.

Do you know what you are aiming for, what matters to you, and what makes you and your family happy? You can choose more than one way to define success. Defining what you really want to be known for (*what will people say about you when you are gone?*) is critical to knowing what your version of success is, so that you can effectively set your sights on it. Until you honestly assess your motivations and desires, your ability to utilize the Five Powers will be incomplete.

So what are the benchmarks or indicators that will tell you when you have arrived at this coveted state of success? It may, indeed, be material wealth and other outward indicators, such as an executive role in a Fortune 500 company. Consciously building kindness capital in your professional life allows you to achieve those pragmatic successes that we all strive for at some level: money, possessions, influence, power, status, and financial security. Most of us want to be outwardly successful—businesspeople in particular. Most people—about 73 percent—reported in a

Gallup Panel Survey that they believed they would be happier if they made more money.[6] There is nothing wrong with that, and, in fact, there is a lot right with it. A healthy desire for achievement is in large part what a successful economy is built on, where innovation comes from, and how advances in health and technology spring forth. Wanting to be the most successful, highest achieving, and most respected you can be is nothing to be ashamed of.

In my lectures, the brainstormed definition of a highly successful person always includes much broader markers than monetary achievement. Balanced, confident, well-liked, resourceful, respected, and happy always come out at the top of the hallmarks of a successful person.

For you, success might be the opportunity to work with your family and friends in an entrepreneurial setting where no one is going to tell you to put on a suit. Perhaps it is a part-time job that pays you well enough to allow you to focus on your hobbies or service to the community. It might be the ability to retire early to write a book. It might be simply defined as being happy, or developing a deeper sense of significance in what you do.

I agree with personal and professional development guru Tony Robbins that "…ultimate power is the ability to produce the results you desire most *and* create value for the other person in the process."[7] As you learn from successful individuals and businesses that have high levels of kindness capital and begin to see your professional life and business flourish, you will wonder why you didn't pursue this path years ago. You will see how the immense force of kindness simultaneously helps you get ahead *and bring others with you.*

Business is not a zero-sum game; you *can* have it both ways. The Five Powers show you how.

Chapter 2

The Power of Reputation

A good reputation is more valuable than money.

—Publilius Syrus

When tallying up our business assets, we often list the tangibles: bank account balance, projected revenues, real property, client list, stock, and equipment. We rarely consider that the most important thing an individual or business can possess is not something that can be counted, filed, ordered, or held.

This most valuable of business assets can work to your advantage or cut your career and business to tatters: your reputation. The impact was immediate when former New York Governor Eliot Spitzer's illicit affairs with prostitutes came to light. It devastated his job, his career, and his family. It was bad enough that his conduct constituted a crime and that he could be charged with conspiracy in the case. But the worst had already happened: it had shattered his reputation. Ronald Woods, a former FBI agent and federal prosecutor, speculated that all the charges possible would not be laid, saying: "...they've already ruined his reputation. It would seem a bit heavy-handed to proceed with a prosecution."[1]

The New Professional

...companies that take social responsibility seriously can improve their business reputations and operational efficiency...

—Arthur A. Thompson Jr., business strategy author

Most business relationships are conducted based on a professional's reputation. So what exactly does "professional" mean, anyway? Historically there were only three professions: ministry, medicine, and the law. Each of these occupations had specific and regulated admittance criteria. Their members were required to profess to higher levels of accountability, and swear oaths to take special care and diligence. These occupations became known for having high standards and their members became highly desirable and influential, partly due to their relative rarity resulting from the rigor of achieving that designation.

Through time, the definition of a profession has greatly expanded and countless occupations are now included. The term *professional* has extended even more and being so labeled is now a more general statement, an adjective descriptive of a high-quality and highly-qualified person. Even as professionalism has generalized and broadened, it remains a very desirable label to achieve in business.

A professional reputation is what you are known for—what people think of when they hear your name, see your company brand, or wish to do business in your field. Professional reputation might center on being reliable, conscientious, highly skilled, or experienced. A computer company will want to be known as innovative with ahead-of-the-curve technologies. A hair salon's image should include high-quality products and modern techniques. A financial institution needs to be seen as full-service, able to conduct a myriad of transactions.

Above any specific niche a business carves out, it must also be known for kindness in order to be a business of choice in the 21st century. Good reputations rise and fall on establishing that you have the best interests of others in mind—that you *care* about them.

Many people genuinely care about others, but fail to match their business practices to their beliefs. Establishing a caring reputation is one of the most compelling, practical reasons for an individual or business to actively be kind. Showing that you are concerned about others' best interests gives you immediate individual and corporate credibility, and puts you in a position to gain many benefits. People don't want to do business with those who are not interested in their outcomes. Think about physicians, estheticians, lawyers, and car salespeople. People prefer to do business with those they trust to care about them.

More important than market share, quality of products or services, or even the lowest prices, a reputation for caring is a critical professional asset, particularly in today's business climate.

The Caring Conundrum

If you do the right thing, you'll be rewarded.

—Carole Black, former president and
CEO of Lifetime Entertainment Services

Many people compare the modern business world unfavorably with the professional climate of yesteryear. The 21st-century business world is much more complex than in years past. Earlier contracts were shorter, agreements were honor-based, and business partners were on the same continent. There is a scarcity of kindness capital and very little expectation of caring in today's business community.

We lack confidence in our leaders and colleagues alike. Although many business and political leaders of the past at least *seemed* to put the satisfaction of their stakeholders first, their equivalent counterparts of today seem to be more concerned with immediate gratification and profit taking—*their* gratification and profits. We are not at all certain that others will keep our best interests in mind and do right by us. We simply don't trust them to care about us.

You need only think of Enron, WorldCom, Tyco, Arthur Andersen, and Adelphia Communications, or of Dennis Kozlowski, Congressman Duke Cunningham, and Governor Elliot Spitzer, to see why confidence in caring is on the decline. CEOs and board chairs take huge bonuses—even when their company loses money. A survey by pollster George Barna approached the question of trust from an ethical perspective.

Respondents were asked how much confidence they had that a variety of leaders would reliably make morally solid decisions on the job. A mere 12 percent of those surveyed trusted executives of large corporations, and elected government officials were perceived poorly too, with only 18 percent having "complete" or "a lot" of confidence in them. When respondents were asked to choose what the root of the corruption in Enron and WorldCom was, 39 percent believed that greed was the cause.[2]

A Harris Poll conducted a couple of years later in 2004 confirmed these dismal results, for both Americans and Europeans. Only 19 percent of Americans trusted trade unions, and the government itself warranted trust by merely 27 percent of Americans and 28 percent of Europeans.[3]

It is not only the general public that harbors this sort of mistrust. Employees themselves do not trust those they work for: less than half of employees surveyed across the United States in 2006/2007 reported having trust and confidence in senior management.[4]

Clearly, we no longer expect professionals to make choices that reflect care or concern about others. Rather, we anticipate that self-interest will rule the decisions and actions of our professional and political leaders alike. Faceless profit-taking can seem inexorably juxtaposed against kindness capital. Needless to say, handshake deals are largely a thing of the past, and this makes people anxious. Remember, people don't want to do business with those who don't have their best interests in mind.

It is in this very era of unabashed self-interest and plummeting public confidence that the Power of Reputation distinguishes you from your competition. Other professionals leave open a void when they fail to cultivate a caring reputation. You can be the exception to the rule—the one professional, the one company that bucks the trend of high-pressure sales, cutthroat deal-making, and carelessness with others' concerns.

Professionals can rely on the Golden Rule principle to guide them through all of their professional dealings in a way that establishes their caring reputation and develops kindness capital for all.

The Golden Approach to Reputation

To many people, the Golden Rule sounds like a soft approach to business. But nothing could be farther from the truth.

—John Maxwell, leadership speaker and author

It can be difficult to identify just how to be kind in business, and more difficult still to see how that route is advantageous. Sorting out the many alternatives and opportunities that arise in our multinational, litigation-favoring, and disparate professional climate is no easy chore. Particularly in tough economic times, knowing how to proceed can be a quandary.

The individual professional needs a rule, a psychological shortcut, to making solid business decisions. The golden rule principle, "do unto others as you would have them do unto you," is a good place to start.

This simple aphorism is not really a religious concept. Although it is based in Christianity and used in one form or another in many other religions and cultures, it is a simple way to approach complex business scenarios.[5] The golden rule avoids moral or political judgments about what is "right" and what is "wrong," and calls instead for a focus on what is "kind." You get a hard and fast answer in most cases, and with that a peace of mind and sense of sureness that is invaluable and increasingly rare. In a world of increasing complexity, uncertainty, and options, peace of mind is no small thing. You will react to business decisions with poise and a strong sense of character, even while others are floundering.

The golden rule is best interpreted as: Treat others only in ways that you are willing to and would like to be treated in the same situation. The reflective nature of the statement—thinking of a decision as if it were being made about you—inserts a critical mirror between decisions guided by genuine care and those of unenlightened self-interest.

Ask yourself how you would like to be treated in any given situation and act accordingly. The customer-service industry would truly be revolutionized if it followed this simple guideline. What client would want to wade through endless voice-message systems without ever reaching a live person to explain her unique situation? What customer would enjoy being stuck on the runway for hours on a stalled airplane with no water? None.

A company's success starts and ends with the individuals who run it, work in it, buy from it, or are served by it. Each individual in a company can choose to act according to the golden rule by treating others—coworkers and customers, competitors and cleaning staff—the way they would like to be treated. When top leadership acts with kindness and respect, they create kindness capital in their organization. Indeed, corporate kindness must be prioritized at the top. Jim Blanchard and J.C. Penney are two such golden-rule type leaders.

Leading With the Golden Rule

Jim Blanchard, CEO of Synovus Financial Corporation, bases his company's reputation for caring on living the golden rule. Listed on *Fortune* magazine's "100 Best Companies to Work For" 10 out of 11 years, with a high-water mark of the top company in 1999, Synovus's approach earns it kudos from its employees. Blanchard believes that the golden rule is really the only rule that a company needs to guide it to success: "The tangible benefits are lower turnover, fewer EEOC claims, almost a disappearance of any kind of harassment issues. But intangible [benefits are that] you keep your best folks, your young emerging leaders want to stay, and people grow and flourish in an environment where they are not suppressed…. Following the Golden Rule is a win-win."[6] As a result, Synovus is a high-return company generating 18.31 percent return on equity in 2006.

J.C. Penney called his stores the "Golden Rule" stores, binding himself publicly to the philosophy that he and his company were about much more than profits. Not that financial success didn't matter, but that profits were not the sole *raison d'etre*. Taught at an early age by his father to be respectful of others, his management philosophy was to hire and train the best people and then put a lot of trust and respect in them, to encourage individual professionals to flourish. He would reward hard work and respect with the opportunity of partnership in a new store location. He fostered his employees and embraced their successes. In turn, his company flourished as his kindness and trust was paid back with hard work and honesty. Focusing on partnerships allowed him to build up enviable profits: "...money is properly the byproduct of building men as partners."[7] J.C. Penney stores expanded across the nation with top talent drawn to its fine reputation for internal promotion and upward career mobility. And its share value continues to flourish under the golden rule principle: in the five years since 2003, J.C. Penney stock has grown by 162 percent.

The golden rule provides a straightforward and easy-to-apply guideline for "on the ground" business decisions. When moving to larger office space, the question of how to allocate the executive offices in the new headquarters naturally arises, and might seem to be a quandary. Who gets the biggest office: you or the other VP? Choosing to allocate office space based on years' seniority, rate of pay, or past achievements only engenders competition and comparisons—and someone has to lose that comparison. The golden rule helps you consider both your hopes and expectations. You acknowledge that he needs office space that makes him comfortable and reflects the achievement he has brought to the company through the course of many years. Recognizing your own desire for the same comfort and dignity, you initiate a conversation about what key features are most important to each of you. He may choose a stellar view as a top criteria, while you may prefer an office that has closer proximity to the board room for easy access to the video-conferencing you frequently do.

The allocation of the executive offices then becomes a relatively easy matter of finding the space that best fits your needs and the other's needs, and allowing each person to have their top priority while compromising on their lesser wants. Choosing to treat others the way you would like to be treated finds the respectful solution that both satisfies and builds your caring reputation.

The golden rule encourages the kind and generous actions that you hope others will do for you, your business, and your loved ones. If you would like someone to hold the door open for you when your arms are full, you need to hold the door open for others. If you would like someone not to spread a rumor about you, you need to refuse to spread rumors you hear, or, better yet, defuse the rumor right on the spot. If you would like help obtaining a promotion, then you would do well to support a colleague who is looking to develop her career.

Bear in mind that the golden-rule reason to be kind is not to obtain an advantage or to get ahead. It would be a mistake to look at the golden rule as a rule of exchange and use it simply to get what you want. It's not "do unto others so they will do unto you."[8] The mindset shifts we looked at earlier ensure that the focus is simply on being kind for the sake of kindness, while incidentally obtaining the benefits of the best business tool around.

John Maxwell, leadership author and speaker, believes that there are two pathways that people can choose in seeking success: "You can go for the gold, or you can go for the Golden Rule."[9] Single-mindedly focusing on wealth and acquisitions is a path that is not going to give you the gold you really seek, especially not in the long term. Rather, the gold will come as you affect the lives of others for the better. Like those successful individuals and companies that have gone before you, you will be kind *and* prosperous.

But I disagree with Maxwell in one key way. You don't have to choose *between* gold and the golden rule. Instead, you can go for the gold *in* the golden rule!

Do so by building an organization- and industry-wide reputation for caring.

Corporate Kindness

Politeness and consideration for others is like investing pennies and getting dollars back.

—Thomas Sowell, economist and author

At first you might think that kindness is the domain of nonprofits and service organizations. Such businesses exist for the purpose of helping others, making kindness and doing good the core of their product or service. Yet corporate kindness works for all companies—whether their primary purpose is profit or investing in the community they serve. Any business, large or small, can create a caring reputation by comprehensively providing the three cores of corporate kindness—volunteerism, charitable giving, and a positive work environment.

Peter Omidyar's approach is: "Business can be a force for good. You can make the world a better place *and* make money." When Peter Omidyar left eBay in 2001, he had amassed a $10-billion fortune from the company he had founded. He moved on to create the Omidyar Network, a company that is both philanthropic yet profit-oriented. Omiydar focuses on microfinance loans to entrepreneurs in developing countries.

These microfinance loans are not charitable donations; rather, they help ordinary people bloom into profitable entrepreneurs. Individuals draw upon and develop their own strengths as they turn these small loans into working livelihoods. The newly successful entrepreneurs pay back their loans with interest. And sometimes the entrepreneurs turn into micro-financiers themselves, continuing the cycle of giving and receiving and giving again, which benefits the individual entrepreneur as well as the community. The Omidyar Network provides a tool for empowerment and poverty eradication while at the same time creating wealth for all of the stakeholders involved.

To be effective, corporate kindness must be institutionalized. It is not just a company mission statement or lofty ideal that establishes a business's caring reputation. What we say *about* ourselves and our businesses is only one indicator, often a poor one, of the esteem in which we are *actually* held. Similarly, having a kind executive or two in the company will not make for a corporate kindness strategy. A caring reputation is necessarily a company-wide identity built—and bought into—by everyone involved. It must be imbued in the mission, vision, values, *and practices* of the company.

Undeniably the world leader in the search engine business, Internet giant Google has corporate kindness figured out. Its reputation for corporate kindness touches customers and employees alike and its success in a very competitive field continues, in large part due to its corporate kindness mission and practices. If Google's mission statement touted good employee relations but failed to make its celebrated employee bikes available, create dynamic workroom environments, and give incentive-creating employee bonuses for new ideas, its claim of "family friendly" would not mean much. Instead, Google's reputation for corporate kindness makes it one of the most sought-after employers in the high-tech industry.

Think of Nordstrom and what immediately comes to mind? Great return policy. Not because it is written down in some rules and procedures manual, but because all of Nordstrom's employees respond with courtesy every day and give each customer the benefit of the doubt on questionable returns. It is the implementation, not the ideology, that builds a reputation of corporate credibility.

Integrate kindness into your company's practices in the way that Tom Peters, leadership and management author recommends: "Commit yourself to performing one new 10-minute act of exceptional customer service every day. Induce your colleagues to do the same. In the course of a year, in a 100-person organization, this will result in 24,000 new acts of kindness and such is the stuff of revolutions."

Successful businesses show that they have all of their stake-holders' best interest in mind—their colleagues, employees, bosses, suppliers, competitors, customers, clients, and even those not directly affected by the business. Yep, caring really does have a place in business. Let's see how professionals can establish their caring reputation in the eyes of their two most important constituents: customers and employees.

Collect and Keep Customers

A good name is more desirable than great riches.

—King Solomon

Professionals and businesses must show they care, both to build a consumer market and to keep existing clients. Be it a multinational company designing automobile components for the mass market or a sole proprietorship creating Websites for individual local businesses, a caring reputation is incredibly influential in drawing new customers, and keeping current ones. A telephone company with infuriatingly poor or rude customer service will not be frequented often, even if its cell phones use all the best technology. The most fashionable clothing store will not see many customers grace its door if brusque employees fail to magnetize new clients. And a bank that does not create trust in the consistent and caring servicing of its clients will be unable to compete in the fast-paced, high-choice finance industry.

Granted, being kind, courteous, and respectful of all customers is a noble end in itself. But gaining the loyalty of customers is absolutely essential for business. It is expensive not to. Extensive research shows that it is five to 12 times more expensive to gain a new customer than to keep an existing one. Studies also indicate that 96 percent of unhappy customers never complain about the poor service that turned them off, but 90 percent of these unsatisfied customers do not buy again nor do they come back.[10]

Creating loyalty in today's business climate can be a daunting proposition. Potential and current customers can choose from a vast array of products and services and have the ability to comparison shop with ease. One factor rises to the top in engendering strong customer loyalty: kindness capital. Investing in your business by treating clients exceptionally well creates customers who will stick with you. Nordstrom, EMC, O'Reilly Public Relations, and L.L. Bean show us how kindness capital elicits customer loyalty.

Taking responsibility for actions, products, and results makes customers feel cared for. This is where Nordstrom really makes its mark. Known for authenticity and quality, it honors its word and cares about its customers—actually puts its customers' needs ahead of its own immediate benefits.

Nordstrom does this by empowering its employees to do virtually whatever it takes to please the customer. One famous urban legend, tells of an elderly gentleman who was permitted to return a set of tires he was dissatisfied with, even though Nordstrom never sold tires. The employee serving the gentleman did not need to put the request through a long chain of command, fill out multiple forms, or promise to get back to him. The employee was able to make a decision on the spot to create a loyal customer by following the Nordstrom Employee

Handbook: "Rule #1—Use your good judgment in all situations. There will be no additional rules." When a company
has this level of established kindness capital, it "owns its customers," in the words of Ed Horrell, author of *The Kindness
Revolution*. Nordstrom's caring reputation and ability to impress and inspire its customers has allowed it to move from
"renting" transient, and easily distracted customers to owning
loyal, committed customers.

When information infrastructure technology company EMC
was a relatively new kid on the block in the late 1980s, things
were not going so well. When a large batch of faulty disc drives
were shipped to EMC customers, the outcry from aggrieved customers who relied on the data storage units required action. Mike
Ruettgers, the then executive vice president of operations and
customer service, made a dramatic move to remedy the problem
and restore customer confidence. He offered each affected customer the choice between a new EMC storage unit or an equivalent one made by their top competitor IBM. Doubtful customers
chose the free IBM units over EMC units by the droves so that
at one point Ruettgers reported shipping more IBM products
than their own. But the tactic worked, customers appreciated
the extraordinary customer service commitment and once the
kinks were worked out, they came back in even bigger droves.
Ruettgers was named CEO in 1992 and the company has thrived
ever since, picking up recognitions and awards for customer service and innovation and becoming one the most successful tech
companies of its kind.[11]

Hopefully you and your company will never have to go to the extremes that EMC did to gain customer loyalty. But you can get in on this customer "stickiness" by finding out what makes your customers tick. Consider a customer satisfaction survey (though beware that these can irritate as much as ingratiate overly inundated consumers). Establish a "customer kindness hotline" with a toll-free number. Make sure that your hotline is staffed by a live person, not an automated system. Publicize it well. Similarly, establish a "customer kindness advisory panel" to meet with customers regularly. [12] You can invite regular customers or use random samples. Don't assume that everyone is on the Internet. Install an old-fashioned customer suggestion box with prominent signage somewhere at your place of business.

Have someone assigned to respond to each suggestion received, even if only to thank them for their thoughts. When a good suggestion from a customer is adopted, publicize it well—in your company newsletter or other mechanisms. Pretty soon your reputation for caring will have smart customers vying to give you the next best marketing tip or customer retention strategy. Remember the words of an anonymous writer who said, "Business will continue to go where invited and remain where appreciated."

As Nordstrom points out, companies build a caring reputation by making kindness to customers the foundation of its success, not a secondary effort. Amazon has such enduring popularity in online book sales that it has been described as "eating eBay's lunch…every one of their competitors' lunches."[13] Attributable, at least partially, to its esteem for its customers, Amazon CEO Jeff Bezos said, "We see our customers as invited guests to a party, and we are the hosts. It's our job every day to make every important aspect of the customer experience a little bit better." Thinking of your customers and clients as invited guests to a party you are throwing changes the dynamic, and lays the foundation for exceptional customer care.

Patrick O'Reilly, owner of O'Reilly Public Relations, knows about building a strong and loyal client base as well. "If you want more money," he said when we met, "serve more people." His Southern California public relations firm thrives—with multi-million dollar profits even in a highly competitive and difficult economy—due to a business philosophy that he immediately identifies as grounded in the golden rule. In an interview, he told me: "You get more when you give more."

His company's core values feature prominently on the wall in the reception area. Smaller plaques featuring those values are also given to each new employee to display at their desks. Two of his company's core values speak directly to kindness—respect and service—and complement his emphasis on results and accountability. "To respect your clients you have to understand their needs and wants," Patrick told me. When you are able to understand where a client is coming from and what he really wants, then you know how to respect and accordingly keep that client. With 90 percent of O'Reilly's new clients coming from satisfied customer referrals, kindness capital clearly works.

Creating customer loyalty is not about eliminating all customer service glitches or creating a perfect process, but rather consistently and uncompromisingly treating customers nicely. The golden rule philosophy of the original owner and namesake of the highly successful outdoor clothing and equipment company, L.L. Bean, shows that a caring reputation is constructed carefully. "A lot of people have fancy things to say about Customer Service, but it's just a day-in, day-out, ongoing, neverending, persevering, compassionate kind of activity," said Leon Gorman, chairman of the board of L.L. Bean. Renowned for its caring, no-questions-asked, customer service reputation, L.L. Bean relies on customer loyalty in differentiating itself from its competitors and contributing to annual sales of $1.5 billion.

When professionals and their companies make a caring reputation a mainstay of their business purpose, they are not only being kind to individual customers but they also get to collect and *keep* customers. Having high levels of kindness capital also means they get to choose among the best and brightest employees in the world.

Don't Buy the Best and Brightest

The end result of kindness is that it draws people to you.

—Anita Roddick, founder and
former CEO of The Body Shop

In an agile labor environment characterized by high choice, mobility, and access to the global marketplace, attracting top-notch employees can be challenging. Fortunately, a business known for caring about its employees will have prime employ-ees flocking to its door.

In fact, you rarely need to "buy" the best and brightest. While compensation is certainly a factor in where highly skilled em-ployees choose to work, corporate culture is often *more* impor-tant than remuneration. More than a third of executives say that work environment and advancement opportunities are the top considerations in evaluating employment opportunities.[14] Simi-larly, 73 percent of respondents to a 2002 Monster.com poll said they would accept less money if they could have a better work environment.

Customers go to Starbucks not only for the good, strong coffee. The haute-casual atmosphere of conversation nooks, soft or lively jazz, and sidewalk bistro tables and comfy chairs all cre-ate a space regularly remarked upon and visited—the "coffeehouse experience." Cornerstone to this environment is the friendly, charming baristas. The casual efficiency and attention to customer care of these dynamic employees are no accident. Starbucks uses corporate kindness to attract and retain the best baristas in the business.

"Starbucks barista" is a highlight on many a young person's resume. Employees migrate to companies that make them feel good about themselves and about their jobs. Starbucks encour-ages its employees to take time to volunteer in their communi-ties through its "Make Your Mark" volunteer program. Volunteer opportunities coupled with enjoyable and sociable work enables Starbucks to choose from many talented individuals to populate its employee ranks.

Starbuck's staff attraction and satisfaction is unprecedented in the service industry. Starbucks' position on the annual list of *Fortune*'s "100 Best Companies to Work For" 10 times in the past 11 years reflects the success of this approach. CEO Howard Schultz posited in his memoir: "We can be extremely profitable and competitive, with a highly regarded brand, and also be respected for treating our people well. In the end, it's not only possible to do both, but you can't really do one without the other."[15]

More important though than what the numbers indicate or the management claims, is what the employees themselves say. My research assistant for this book, Kristin Walder, was once a Starbucks barista. Kristin told me that "the expectation was that we would be positive and friendly for the sake of the customers. But as a result, the employees felt happy and upbeat too and that made it a great place to work. The experience really made me more outgoing, more of a people-person. I loved it!" Record-high employee satisfaction in turn makes stopping by Starbucks a pleasant experience for the customer; a key factor that results in remarkably high customer loyalty.

As the Starbucks experience exemplifies, businesses become talent magnets when they are known for excelling in the three cores of corporate kindness: providing their employees with opportunities to volunteer and make an impact in the community; having a healthy philanthropy practice that makes people proud to be associated with the company; and, creating a caring and creative workplace environment in which people compete to work. Let's take a closer look at each of these three elements.

Employees Making an Impact

...negative employees can scare off every customer they speak with - for good.

—Tom Rath, author

Employees need to feel involved—to make a contribution that makes them feel engaged, respected, and valued. Adaptable 21st-century professionals and corporations have caught on to community involvement as a method of creating a contented, motivated workforce. Companies such as Dell Computers, Gap Inc., and L.L. Bean are increasingly not only permitting, but actively encouraging, their employees to volunteer. Many companies are providing incentives for their employees' community efforts, including time off, matching donations, and other perquisites.

In a competitive global economy, marketing dollars only go so far. Businesses are also beginning to recognize that doing volunteer work not only makes for a good employee attraction and retention tool, it also shines a positive light on company image and corporate brand. Companywide volunteer efforts are on the rise. Technology and communications giant Ericsson Canada gives employees three days off annually to volunteer, and will also donate $200 to any charity where an employee volunteers at least 60 hours in one year. CitiGroup and IBM do it too.

Launched in 2006, and repeated in 2007, multinational financial corporation CitiGroup held a "Global Community Day" in which more than 50,000 volunteers from its bank branches in 100 countries, all wearing T-shirts emblazoned with the CitiBank logo, made a day-long effort to care for the poor and enrich the environment. Ensuing media coverage of the CitiBank volunteer efforts resulted in invaluable goodwill and public relations.

IBM has established an online mechanism to inform and encourage its employees to invest themselves in volunteer activities. IBM's director of corporate community relations, Diane Melley, notes that when their people volunteer, it not only makes a difference to that community, but that "it also enables our people to get the IBM brand out there and to spread some of our technology which is also very beneficial to the business." There is nothing wrong with that attitude.

In fact, to remain competitive, companies are finding that they *must* offer such opportunities to attract top talent. Tim Riley, head of personnel at the marketing firm Forrester Research, notes that the opportunity to volunteer is a priority for many people seeking professional positions. He links it to today's values: "I think it reflects a shift in people, younger people who want to work in a company whose values are similar to their own."

The result of providing volunteer opportunities to employees? The savvy, community-oriented company gets more satisfied, better networked, and more loyal staff.

Many companies have found that the second major tenant of corporate kindness—philanthropy—is an even better way to impress upon employees, and other stakeholders, that they care.

Practicing Philanthropy

Giving truly is the highest level of living. It makes the world a better place. And it also makes for better business.

—John C. Maxwell

Initially counterintuitive, giving away money is an excellent business strategy to build a companywide or individual caring reputation. Philanthropy is an investment for businesses—an investment in their caring reputation from which they can rightly anticipate both short- and long-term returns.

Much corporate giving centers on the creation of a caring reputation. Author Arthur Brooks examined charity in America and found that "philanthropy is really motivated by trying to build a reputation in the community."[16] For the individual professional, giving is part of your reputation too. It establishes you in your community as someone who cares and is trusted to have the best interests of others at heart.

A top independent bookstore in the nation, Vroman's Bookstore in Southern California makes kindness and philanthropy a mainstay of its business and sees many benefits from doing so. Its reputation for caring truly precedes it. I was referred to Vroman's by a number of individuals who insisted I must learn about this great bookstore in my research for this book. Vroman's corporate kindness program has origins that go back as far as 1894 to its original owner. It includes a profit-sharing plan for employees, an employee enrichment program of learning opportunities, a go-green initiative, and a giving campaign for a local children's organization during the holidays. Attracted by Vroman's kindness-based business philosophy, president and COO Allison Hill accepted this management position several years ago. Many employees have since told Allison that the employee-centric approach made the difference in their choices, too.

The Vroman's Gives Back program is the centerpiece of how it makes doing good a great business strategy. Vroman's contributes 1 percent of each sale to a charitable organization of the customer's choice. Nearly half a million dollars have been given back to local charities, creating not only tremendous good for the charities but also remarkable local goodwill for Vroman's. It makes employees feel good about joining the company. But does this philanthropy also matter to the book-buying customer?

You bet it does.

Vroman's survey of 1,500 customers proved what they had already suspected: 70 percent said that the program greatly influenced their choice to shop, and continue to shop, at Vroman's.

Allison Hill was gratified when they were recognized as the 2008 Bookseller of the Year by *Publishers Weekly*. Allison's enthusiasm for giving back to the community could not be contained when she told me about their presentation to the *Publishers Weekly* selection panel. Presenting on a number of required categories, including innovation and financials, Allison's team emphasized the community involvement category and feels that made the difference in obtaining this prestigious industry recognition. Vroman's balances a focus on profitability with doing good for its employees and in its community. "Our philosophy is to be profitable and successful while creating a microcosm of goodness. We strive to make our little piece of the world in Vroman's better than the bigger world," said Allison.

When many bookstores are struggling to hold on to their market share, sales of $13.5 million annually makes Vroman's one of the top-grossing independent bookstores in the United States.

Opportunities for volunteerism and charitable giving practices thus contribute to a caring reputation that impresses employees and other stakeholders. Employees are also drawn to employers that exhibit high levels of kindness capital through positive work environments.

Employee Environment

People just want to know that somebody knows, and cares.

—Dennis P. LeStrange,
former senior VP of IKON Office Solutions

Creating workplace environments rife with kindness capital is a 21st-century workforce imperative. We already saw that employees will often opt for a positive environment over a higher salary. Now let's see how such an employer becomes a talent magnet.

Patagonia, the Southern Californian–based outdoor clothing and equipment seller with more than 1,000 employees spanning 39 stores in seven countries, practices corporate kindness. Patagonia's ethos of fun work, respect, and corporate caring for its employees is paired with a commitment to producing the highest quality, environmentally friendly products.

Written by Patagonia founder and chairman Yvon Chouinard the *Let My People Go Surfing* book outlines the company's corporate commitment for caring. For Chouinard and his people, kindness and caring is more than a mission statement, it is a mission. Thought to have perhaps "…the best reputation in the industry even while it faces increasing competition from much larger companies," Patagonia has fostered loyalty and built an enviable worldwide reputation. "Most people want to do good things, but don't. At Patagonia, it's an essential part of your life," said Chouinard.[17]

Consistently featured on *Fortune*'s "100 Best Companies to Work For" list, Patagonia has given out $22 million in cash and in-kind donations from 1985 to 2005. To ensure it attracts and retains top-performing employees, Patagonia offers a variety of lifestyle benefits to its employees. Benefits range from encouraging employees to get out there and enjoy a good surf, onsite daycare, compensating for part of college expenses, and offering sabatticals to employees to do environmental work. Committing to employee satisfaction means employees are committed to putting their all into a day's work. With 900 resumes on average received for each job opening, Patagonia indeed gets the top talent.

Patagonia does have high expectations for performance. It demands, and receives, results: this privately held company sees operating margins at the high end of the industry average and earns about $230 million per year.

A caring reputation is especially important with the recognition that reputation doesn't spread quickly: it is viral.

Viral Reputation

A good name, like good will, is got by many actions and lost by one.
—Lord Jeffery

When my husband, John, and I decided to buy a boat, it was a foray into a whole new world. Boating, we found, is a fun and wonderful experience. It is also a world rife with confusing lingo, new problems, and specialized services. In the purchase process, we relied entirely on our boating friends. They told us about the best brands, what qualities to avoid, and which boat brokers could be trusted. Once we bought the boat, we relied on referrals from our boat broker to decide who would do the boat survey; where to take it for servicing, washing, and waxing; which insurance company to use; and where to shop for the parts and accessories it seems to need endlessly. Reputation, spread by word-of-mouth referrals, was *the* deciding factor in our entire purchase process.

Failing to cultivate a caring reputation can be fatal. A salesperson who does not persuade that she cares about the customer's best interests will find that the customer simply moves on—and takes her friends and neighbors with her. In our boating foray, one skeptical remark or arched eyebrow from our trusted sources made us flee in the other direction from doubtful service providers.

In an economic environment that is remarkable for its multiplicity of choices and ease of shopping, reputation is more important now than ever before. Many of us have more than one option for employment; we can hire from pools of hundreds of enthusiastic grads. We can buy, watch, or enjoy countless products and services. Our reach is nearly limitless—across oceans and around the world. Technology has brought connectedness to a new level and opportunity along with it. Job opportunities are the click of a button away. We need not settle for bad customer service, a substandard employee, or an inequitable employment situation. We can, and we do, move. And we move rapidly.

The power of reputation is thus incredibly potent. Your reputation is common news, and it spreads like wild fire. Instant feedback on your actions and performance (you are likely to be caught on a cell phone camera, show up on YouTube, Angie's List, or a blog) means that your reputation is indeed public knowledge. The extreme transparency of the modern day underscores the litmus test for any business actions. It is sometimes referred to as the newspaper headline test—would you be willing to see your action splashed across the front page of the newspaper or across the screens of countless computers around the world? Your decisions, both small and large, are seen and judged by innumerable others.

What's more, customers who feel disrespected, or "dissed," will often use all the technology tools at their disposal to vent their frustration and actively hurt your business. *BusinessWeek*'s editor-in-chief Steven L. Adler, offered the lessons of companies with good customer service records as a way to "…avoid the dangerous slipups that can drive today's digitally empowered customers to trample a brand's name across the internet."[18]

Hotels that misrepresent themselves in advertising are thwarted by Websites that have proliferated in recent years. For one, TripAdvisor.com allows instantaneous posts of visitor comments about their hotel stays. If a hotel wants repeat business, it knows that the individual expecting a tranquil stay, yet woken up in the middle of the night by the disco next door, is not just a single lost client but representative of all the people who read the scathing remarks posted by the bleary-eyed client the next morning. The hotel's reputation is better served when it tips off its guests that they are not likely to find a spa-like environment and instead promises a "lively and boisterous" neighborhood with plenty of entertainment options.

The fragility of a good reputation is well stated by Warren Buffett: "It takes 20 years to build a reputation and 5 minutes to ruin it." Without a good reputation, you don't have much.

Politicians understand this better than most. "Everything's wrapped up in your reputation," said Goeffrey VanderPal, a political candidate for Nevada State Treasurer. He suffered blog attacks lambasting him for running for office after declaring bankruptcy. After losing the 2006 election, and unable to rid himself of the blog postings sullying his reputation, he saw his business opportunities as a financial planner flounder. Reputation management firms have sprouted up in the public relations field, helping those with sullied reputations clean up their Web presence to avoid continued loss of business.

You can also capitalize on these same electronic tools to build your reputation for caring by showing customers and employees what you have to offer. Take advantage of the connectedness and visibility of the Internet and be sure to post your successes to boost your reputation.

A caring reputation is like a well-placed investment that pays dividends in the creation of business opportunities and referrals. Invest well.

Kindness Inhibitor:
The Busyness Barrier

...time is one of the biggest enemies of kindness.

—Margot Silk Forrest, author

I am just too busy to develop an employee volunteer-incentive package. Or, pick up coffee for my secretary. Or, train my employees in golden rule-based customer service. Or, _____ (*You fill in the blank.*) Undoubtedly, there are many things in your action-packed days that you *wish* you could get to.

My mom, Pat, a busy and dynamic school teacher, and I would excitedly recite a mantra as I was growing up: "There's not enough time!" We always said it in mock jest, but now, as a professional myself I feel the time-pinch even more acutely. It is so easy to fall into the trap of thinking that time dictates your choices. In the face of other necessities, kindness often gets pushed to the last on your list of daily activities. Avoiding that trap will help you to recognize that you do have enough time for whatever you choose to be your priorities. The "I'm too busy" excuse is really a way of saying "It's not a priority" or "I'm not that interested."

Even if your own inclination is not currently toward daily kindness (*I can't be bothered. I'm too focused on making a living. No one responds anyway.*), you too can learn to integrate kindness into your life. There are many ways to "sneak" small kindnesses into your business life to build your reputation for kindness. Making kindness a conscious daily choice in your professional and personal life is fundamental to capitalizing on kindness. The dividends that result when you build your reputation at the office will be tremendous. If you are the boss, you'll engender loyalty and enthusiasm among your staff. As a coworker, your team members will undoubtedly rally to you when you need to lean on them. If you are a junior just making your mark, your opportunities are enhanced as you develop your reputation for thoughtfulness and kindness.

I have fallen prey to the busyness barrier more than once. My friend and colleague's elderly mother-in-law was going into hospice care at Christmas time one year and was not expected to recover. When my friend had to stop carpooling temporarily so that she could be more available for the care of her mother-in-law and to be there for her husband, I lost touch with her. I certainly sympathized greatly for their coming loss. I intended to keep in touch, to drop by with food, to keep her posted on workplace happenings.

But a particularly busy time of my life interceded, including the Christmas holidays, a trip with my mother, and a hectic work schedule, combined with the writing of this book. You know how the litany of excuses goes. Suddenly more than a month had passed, and I had not called or checked in with my friend to even offer my support. When I finally came out of my preoccupied, self-absorbed fog of activity that had focused on my own immediate needs, I found out that the mother-in-law had died and that a very hard time had followed.

I did the best I could to make up for my lack of attentiveness, sending a card and following up regularly after that. Like any real friend, she did not hold it against me and we soon were back to our regular carpool schedule. But I knew that I had disappointed her, and myself.

Inspired by ethics expert Michael Josephson's "Be a Better Person Diet," the busyness barrier is no match for the "Be a Kinder Person Program." It will make others feel great and, through quick and easy methods, develop your professional reputation for caring.

- Begin on Monday with encouragement. Pay attention to your coworkers and colleagues and see who is in need of a little boost. Be like my colleague Brenda Flowers and ask someone "How can I make your day better?" and then try to do what they tell you would help them. Pay them a compliment by noting their contribution to a recent project, or by encouraging them to keep going on the tough one they are grappling with. Watch them shine with your positive comments and tackle the project with new vigor.

- On Tuesday, be a model of courtesy. Go out of your way to hold the door open for others, even if it means delaying for a few seconds to wait for that person dashing in to make it to work on time. Make a pot of coffee on your floor at the office and let your colleagues know a fresh pot is ready for them. Note how the smiles you receive in return make you feel good too.

- Wednesday is a day for mentoring and coaching. Take note of juniors in your office environment and offer your help. Be respectful of their boundaries but let them know you are willing to spend some time with them guiding them through the learning experience. Take a junior out for coffee and hear what is on his or her mind. Watch that person blossom into a trusted colleague and ally.

- Inspire someone on Thursday. Send an inspirational quote via e-mail to someone who you know would appreciate it. Lift their thoughts above the mundane, and help them see how their small contributions at the office are making a larger impact. When going through a drive-through at a coffee shop or fast food restaurant, pay for the person behind you. See how your small acts of kindness will inspire others to do the same.

- As the week closes, use Friday to be generous. Bring some fruit to the office and put it in a big bowl in the common room. Tidy up after your colleagues before they have time to worry about it. Share the credit for a major project success. Notice how your generosity is appreciated, and returned.

◈ On the weekend, you can rest. (Though you may want to try out some of these kindness techniques at home too!)

Building your reputation for caring, or the corporate kindness legacy of your company, is not complicated. Give it a try.

Practice Pointers

You can't build a reputation on what you're going to do.

—Henry Ford

To get started building your caring professional reputation, do at least one kind act each week. Pick anything from the "Be a Kinder Person Program" or this list of Practice Pointers and do it. Next week, try doing two kind things. When you see how quick and easy it really is, you can then tackle more acts or ones with greater impact:

◈ Say please, thank you, and excuse me regularly, frequently, and unceasingly. Do this at work and at play. Even if you feel a little silly at first, your colleagues and personal contacts will appreciate it.

◈ At the end of each week, when you are driving home from work on Friday, take a moment to reflect back on the week. Did you develop your reputation for caring? If not, what simple things can you commit to doing next week?

- Target an unhappy coworker and see if you can make him or her feel better.

- If humor is natural for you, use it to make people feel good around you. (Avoid sarcastic or biting tones and watch for appropriateness.)

- Keep your appointments. If you have to cancel, do it with as much advance notice as possible.

- If you say you are going to do something, follow through until it is done.

- Be consistent—be the same person at home and at the office.

- Find time, even just 15 minutes, to sit down in person with your employees and colleagues. Try a rotating schedule but be sure to give each person some "face time" with you.

- At an upcoming staff meeting, raise the topic of kindness and how to create a caring reputation. Get their thoughts on quick and easy ways to do it.

- Make a list in your staff's personnel files keeping track of the good things they do. As they occur to you, jot down even the small things. When evaluation time comes you will be able to easily thank them for their efforts and accomplishments throughout the year.

- Conduct an "act-of-kindness-conspiracy." With other collaborators, pour goodwill, assistance, and appreciation on any colleague, staff member, or business associate that is negative or difficult to work with, and watch his or her attitude change before your eyes.[19]

* Take a colleague, customer, or staff member to lunch.

* Above all, take action. Don't let the busyness barrier get in the way of building your caring reputation.

Your caring reputation will indeed become one of your most prized possessions when you see how much caring about others in business benefits them...and you. Equally powerful, reciprocity is also one of the most reliable results of kindness.

Chapter 3

The Power of Reciprocity

Kindness works. It's like a boomerang; it ALWAYS comes back to you, even if not from the person you gave it to.

—Gayle King

Dr. James "Jim" Erickson, a vice chancellor emeritus at the University of California, Riverside, has countless people who fall over themselves for the chance to return some of the many kindnesses he has bestowed on them so naturally and so casually throughout the years. While he does it without thought of re-payment, he has an enormous reserve of reciprocity—a line-up of supporters waiting at his virtual door step.

When the University of California considered calling him out of semi-retirement to become the interim chancellor of the Riverside campus, an outpouring of support came from com-munity members as they rallied to endorse him. Letters, e-mails, and personal phone calls to the decision-makers flooded in, touting Jim's achievements and character. As one of Jim's closer friends, I received dozens of calls from people asking how they could help. A team of business leaders drove to Los Angeles for a personal meeting with the president of the University of California to advocate for Jim. An informal committee was formed to promote Jim's hiring.

But Jim had not even asked for help. He didn't make a call or send an e-mail. In his usual self-effacing manner, he had kept this opportunity relatively quiet. For Jim, reciprocity meant that he didn't even need to ask for a favor before that favor was granted.

As Jim learned, kindness to others is always returned. Kindness is an investment, and each small kindness accrues to your account of kindness capital. But how?

Reciprocity happens when a kindness extended becomes a kindness returned. Reciprocity is the reward for the care, appreciation, and kindness shown toward others. You throw out a kindness, and it returns to you—a sort of reciprocity "boomerang." You can think of this as positive payback: the creation of business advantages as favors are paid back in kind. This positive payback occurs when your helping hand to a colleague or your consideration to a competitor returns as a courtesy the next time around. Each small kindness returns dividends in your professional life as you build kindness capital.

Another kind of reciprocity returns indirectly and unpredictably, and yet is very powerful. A kind act may go veering off in haphazard directions, getting picked up again and returned in a completely unexpected way, often from a totally different source. More homing pigeon than boomerang, this form of "pay-it-forward" reciprocity often goes unrecognized but is incredibly contagious.

Let's look first at the positive paybacks you can expect to harvest as you plant the seeds of kindness in your professional life.

Reciprocity Reserve

It is a way of buffering yourself from an uncertain future. You never know when you might need help. When you have friends, you're much better off.

—Jay Phelan, evolutionary biologist and author

Nice professionals frequently find themselves on the receiving end of reciprocity, as others reciprocate for their many small and large kindnesses. The golden rule–style of business means generously doing good things for other people and treating them as you would like to be treated. But what the golden rule (incidentally, sometimes referred to as the Reciprocity Rule) doesn't say, at least not explicitly, is that if you want confidence that nice things will be done for you in the future, then you should build up your "reciprocity points" in the present.

Kindnesses build reciprocity points now for redeeming later, just as Jim unintentionally accumulated during the course of many years. This is your kindness capital, a sort of reciprocity reserve account, to draw on when needed.

Sure, you could simply rely on people coming through for you because they too believe in and practice the golden rule. I see so much kindness each day that it is easy to see how an optimist would fail to bother gathering reciprocity points for some distant future need. But why leave it to chance? Especially now in the 21st century, where there is no such thing as predictability in life—and certainly not in the business world.

It won't take long for the uncertain future to arrive at your doorstep. While you might be happy in your position right now, it might not be your ultimate dream job. You may have more than enough clients at the moment, but when the real estate boom of the late 1990s became the early 2000s' bust, many a real estate agent felt the sudden pinch. You may want to expand your horizons, transition to an entirely different career, attract more clients, or follow your spouse's job opportunity to a whole new city.

When the various shifts and turns happen in your life (*aren't they afoot already?*), you will be turning to the very same people with whom you now work and do business. They will be there to put in a good word for you or to help you put your best foot forward in an all-important interview. They will connect you with a new supplier when yours has suddenly declared bankruptcy. They will get you the "friends and family" rate for the convention you are responsible for booking. Remember that your coworker today is the VP of the competitor's company next year. Your colleagues, even mere acquaintances, people with whom you transact business, will be there for you.

Or, at least you hope they will.... The only way to have complete confidence is to build up your kindness capital now. If you *intentionally* shore up your kindness capital, then when help is critically needed, or opportunities arise, you will be guaranteed that people will indeed go out of their way for you. So, if you stay late one evening to help out a coworker with a deadline, you can pretty much be assured that he will stay late for you at some point in the future. That person will be that much more likely to cut into his own personal time to discover the inside track on that job opportunity you are coveting or put his reputation on the line to recommend you to one of his long-established clients.

To put the traditional boomerang effect of kindness into play in your life as you build a reciprocity reserve, there are relatively easy things you can do in your professional life. Take every opportunity to spread goodwill among your colleagues, acquaintances, suppliers, and even competitors. Write a letter of recommendation to help them get that seat on a prestigious board, donate some of your vacation time to an ailing coworker, or alert your boss to a staff member's birthday when she may have forgotten. Do favors for people *before* they ask for help.

Now this might start to sound like a giant chess game. What is my next move, and how can I maximize my benefits versus my colleague's likely actions? But it is really not that complicated. We have already established that all acts of kindness are positive, even when the motive is not *solely* to benefit others. Building kindness capital benefits everyone.

Engineers working for telecommunications firms near San Francisco prove this point. A study of helpfulness patterns among coworkers found that those employees who swapped help—helped others out and correspondingly received help in return—were more productive and more well-regarded by their peers.[1] Like a stable long-term investment, stockpile your reciprocity points now, when you *don't* need them.

We've already seen how it worked for Jim Erickson. Now let's see how kindness to others operates beyond positive payback, as pay-it-forward reciprocity.

Kindness Is Contagious

When you are kind to someone in trouble, you hope they'll remember and be kind to someone else. And it'll become like a wildfire.

—Whoopi Goldberg

The touching book and movie *Pay It Forward* did not script a happy ending but nonetheless sparked an international pay-it-forward phenomenon. Paying-it-forward starts by an unsolicited and unexpected act of doing something good for someone else. The kindness is then reciprocated—*but to someone else altogether.*

Pay-it-forward kindness, also known as "gifting forward" or "serial reciprocity," is contagious. People respond to kindness by proliferating kindness and helpfulness to others. Pay-it-forward kindness is just like chain mail, only without the irritation and intrusion. As recipients of kindness pass it on to others, a chain of kindness is created. Or, more accurately, a web of kindness given and received, forms and spreads.

Kindness paid forward reshapes not only our individual experiences but builds kindness capital and diffuses a "glow of goodwill," affecting our personal, professional, and even global interactions.

How does this happen? A series of foundational experiments have shown how the kindness contagion works.

The "glow of goodwill" is the warmth, positiveness, and good feeling created when receiving even the simplest everyday kindness, such as being given a cookie. In a keystone 1976 psychology experiment, subjects who randomly received a cookie were found to be more likely to participate in an *unrelated* volunteer assignment than those who had not received a cookie. The events seemed unconnected. The subsequent volunteer assignment was not expressly tied to the receipt of the cookie, and the cookie-giver and the volunteer-requester were entirely different people. The volunteer-requester did not refer to the cookie received earlier. It was simply a kind act that created a serial reciprocity. The cookie-receiver was subconsciously motivated to pay-it-forward. "The charity of a stranger, in the form of shared cookies, energized a glow of goodwill," said Professor Harvey Hornstein in his foundational book on aggression versus altruism, *Cruelty & Kindness: A New Look at Aggression and Altruism.* In this way, the glow of goodwill spills over into future and apparently unrelated actions and events. [2]

Follow-on experiments have shown that reciprocity appears, and spreads rapidly, in many other settings. In one test, women shopping in Madison, Wisconsin, who voluntarily completed a questionnaire were either treated kindly with expressed appreciation for their time and effort or, conversely, were not treated nicely at all. Those treated with appreciation were twice as likely to later donate bus fare to a needy person than those who were not treated nicely.[3] Kindness expressed by the appreciative interviewer cast a forward goodwill glow onto the subjects' future actions.

You'll see more in a future chapter about how thanking triggers the tremendous Power of Thanks by meeting our need for appreciation and recognition.

While not especially predictable, pay-it-forward kindness has some very practical applications. The Dane County TimeBank in Wisconsin is a thriving chapter of the international "TimeBanks" organization. In TimeBanks, people help each other and receive credits for their service. Individuals register and describe the abilities and interests that they would be happy to donate—be it accounting, plumbing, painting, or tutoring math. Donations of time are recorded for each member. One hour of time is worth one virtual TimeBank dollar, and these dollars are redeemable for receiving services from other TimeBank members.

TimeBanks use the pay-it-forward principle. Person A might baby-sit for person C, and C might paint the house of H, while H then does the tax return of A eight months later.

TimeBank members know when they sign up and donate their time that they may in fact receive services of lesser value, or may never receive a service in return at all. TimeBank member B might donate several hours of his time mowing lawns for neighbors but never receive the singing lessons he hopes for because that expertise is not in the TimeBank. However, the lawn mower's good services cutting a neighbor's grass spreads goodwill, builds his own stock of kindness capital, and makes connections and establishes friendships where only strangers previously existed. With more than 300 TimeBanks worldwide in 22 countries and 100,000 members, a lot of people are paying-it-forward.

You cannot contain the glow of goodwill, but you can intentionally and purposefully spread it. You can create a kindness contagion in your office or establish a glow of goodwill that surrounds your professional brand. Think of how a glow of goodwill could revolutionize your professional life. You become a talent magnet, drawing the most desirable employees to your business when they see and sense the kindness capital in your workplace. Customers and clients too are magnetized to you, drawn in by the kindness capital that marks your business, your professional brand, and you.

Set the kindness contagion in motion by simply picking from and implementing any of the Practice Pointers at the end of this chapter. *Whenever* you choose to be kind you are triggering the kindness contagion.

The business community has picked up on the contagious nature of paying-it-forward. Hilton Hotels' commitment to hospitality harkens back to founder Conrad Hilton's 1919 philosophy of kindness and warmth. Indeed for Hilton, as for any hotel, hospitality is their business, their *raison d'etre*. But Hilton has taken it further and deeper than most, and in 2006 launched a "be hospitable" campaign to ramp up their efforts. Internal training and communications were redesigned to encourage and inspire their 150,000 employees to extend simple gestures of common courtesy to all of the clients they serviced. Their goal: that their many small kindnesses to customers would result in hospitable acts being carried forward.

Hilton also launched an index—an innovative advertising campaign meant to celebrate and promote kind, hospitable acts from around the globe. On the Website they indexed and mapped kind acts as people from around the world logged on to report kindnesses they had seen or participated in. The site even high-lighted particularly poignant or meaningful stories through short videos and vignettes.

Stories ranged from the everyday (helping a stranded traveler locate their car in a big parking lot) to the profound (finding redemption in a small act of generosity). By raising kindness to the level of an international campaign, Hilton Hotels raised aware-ness of kindness and helped to encourage and inspire kind acts.

Not incidentally, Hilton Hotels received considerable posi-tive attention. Hilton Hotels knows that the Power of Reciprocity means that shining the light on kindness is not a one-way street. Pushing its brand to the front of the mind of the many thou-sands of people who have viewed their Website means that they receive the benefits of generating all this kindness—in sales and brand recognition.

The glow of goodwill from paying-it-forward ultimately shines on you as well as your business, as kindness capital builds and grows. Sounds like a good enough reason to foster kindness and reap the benefits of reciprocity? Well, what if you knew that those very same acts of kindness that help others and advance your career will simultaneously, and instantaneously, make you feel happier too?

Helpers Get Happy

Those who bring sunshine to the lives of others cannot keep it from themselves.

—Sir James Barrie, dramatist and author

Do you want to be happy? While it might seem like a frivolous question (*of course I want to be happy*), it is one worth asking and answering thoughtfully for yourself.

Some years back, I attended an ethics seminar for elected and appointed officials by noted ethicist Michael Josephson. He posed a question to the audience: "If you saved the life of a leprechaun and he granted you one wish for your children, what would you choose; (a) enormous wealth, (b) fabulous good looks, (c) superb athletic ability, (d) great fame, or (e) genuine happiness? Naturally, everyone in the audience laughed out loud at the absurdity of the question. Of course you would want your children to have genuine happiness over any of the other superficial manifestations of success. Genuine happiness refers to the more sustainable type that comes from a balanced life ripe with satisfaction and contribution, rather than the fleeting sensations and short-lived "fun" of pleasure-seeking behaviors. Fortunately, kindness can get you there.

Nice people are happier people. Do you agree with the statement? Consider it for a moment. Think of your own life, friends, and family, and consider whether this is evident in your own immediate social environment. How about at work? Is your boss or coworker both nice and happy? (If so, you are fortunate indeed.)

Do you know even a single person who is very nice and considerate but also very unhappy? I suggest that you would be hard-pressed to find such a person. The "helper's high" explains why.

Often equated with the runner's high, being kind gives you a "high." You experience rushes of euphoria and goodwill every time you do something nice for someone else.

Coined by Allan Luks, a researcher at Australia's Curtin University, research revealed that 90 percent of subjects experienced at least one physical or emotional sensation, such as euphoria and increased energy, immediately after doing something kind.[4] It is a special feeling of warm well-being and energy.

And this particular high, unlike the high that comes from artificial substances, brings the kind of euphoria that lasts and builds and has absolutely no negative side effects. In fact, kindness makes you happier *and* healthier. When you consciously increase your kindness capital, you will be less stressed out, have better levels of energy, sleep better, and live longer. Significant numbers of Luks's subjects felt stronger and more energetic, and 13 percent even experienced a reduction in physical aliments such as aches and pains.

Well-being, then, is *another* benefit to you when you help others and gain the benefits of reciprocity. The helper's high comes at least partially from a boost in your self-esteem—you like and respect yourself more when you have done something good. Remarkably, when you take the focus off of what you want and instead focus on what others might want and need, you end up happy. So volunteer at a local charity, help out a colleague, or hold open that door. Edwin Arlington Robinson, three-time Pulitzer Prize winning poet, notes the incredible glow of goodwill we feel when we choose to do something kind: "Two kinds of gratitude: The sudden kind we feel for what we take; the larger kind we feel for what we give."

There are so many benefits to being kind that you'll have to remind yourself that you are doing it for *someone else*. You can try to be selfless by the giving of your time, efforts, and money to help others, but you *still* benefit—substantially and repeatedly.

The "nice guys finish last" myth and the related "no good deed goes unpunished" rumor are two of the most persistent, misinformed beliefs around. When uncorrected, they can hamper even well-intentioned people from embracing kindness and experiencing reciprocity.

Kindness Inhibitor:
The Nice Guys Finish Last Myth

…nice is the toughest four-letter word you'll ever hear.
—Linda Kaplan Thaler and Robin Koval

The proverbial nice guy…ignored, trampled on, and unsuccessful? When "no good deed goes unpunished" is preached as a sort of business gospel, is being cutthroat just an unfortunate necessity in the business world today? Not a chance! Nice guys are typically at the top of the pack, first in line for promotions, on the "A list" for invitations, and generally able to accomplish their wildest dreams. Think rock star Bono, Magic Johnson, and clothing designer Eileen Fisher. Each is known for being kind, generous, likeable, and thoughtful. That is, nice. Each is reaping the benefits of their talents compounded by their niceness.

And yet, inherent in the label "nice" dwells a stigma, or stereotype, that implies weakness. When I was younger, especially while a teenager, if someone commented that I was "sooo nice," I would cringe. *Even I* was concerned with being seen as uninteresting, bland, or a pushover, if I were nice.

Sandra Bullock is a nice person. Known in Hollywood for her legendary kindness, she has donated millions to help others in need. She gave a million dollars to the tsunami-relief effort, stimulating giving by others, without seeking publicity. But she is anything but a pushover. In addition to her reputation for kindness, Bullock is known as a multifaceted talent and business force. She produces, directs, and acts in enormously successful film and TV productions, consistently pulling in the kind of dollars that few stars can claim. Bullock derives a lot of satisfaction from being considered very nice, but acknowledges that societal labeling of niceness is a downside, saying, "It makes me feel good. I love it. I wouldn't change anything. I know sometimes nice becomes synonymous with boring...."[5]

In many ways, this entire book is a counter-argument to the nice guys finish last myth. To really banish this most prevalent myth and build kindness capital, it is necessary to further revamp our mindsets and to strike a healthy balance.

Zero-Sum Game

Life to me is the greatest of all games. The danger lies in treating it as a trivial game, a game to be taken lightly, and a game in which the rules don't matter much. The rules matter a great deal. The game has to be played fairly or it is no game at all. And even to win the game is not the chief end. The chief end is to win it honorably and splendidly.

—Sir Ernest Shackleton, late 19th-century Antarctic explorer

The zero-sum attitude is one reason why the nice guys finish last myth is so pervasive and hard to shake. In the zero-sum world, a gain by one party results in a corresponding loss by another. You can't win unless another loses. Some of the most popular leisure games operate this way. Chess, poker, and Monopoly are zero-sum games—your gaining of a point means the person you are playing with must correspondingly lose a point.

Many businesses play that way, too. Their search for profits means that another company cannot profit. They see clients as limited, resources as scarce, and opportunities as rare. During times of economic downturn, this is particularly insidious.

Zero-sum typifies the world of the legal profession. In litigation, typically one party is deemed "right" and therefore wins, while the other is found "wrong" and loses. While mediation and arbitration are often options in settling lawsuits, and sometimes result in more give-and-take, litigation still operates in the zero-sum realm.

Successful 21st-century businesses recognize that a quick profit in the absence of care and consideration is not desirable and really not often achievable. "Managing only for profit is like playing tennis with your eye on the scoreboard and not on the ball" said Ken Blanchard and Dr. Norman Vincent Peale in their book *The Power of Ethical Management.* If you, or your business, focus only on quick success, superficial fixes to problems, and have a zero-sum attitude, then you fail to cultivate relationships that will sustain you, bring repeat business, and draw positive attention to you.

The zero-sum mentality is a limiting one in business. We must let go of it in order to succeed in the 21st century.

Paradoxically, the *best* time to emphasize kindness strategies (like a caring reputation and reciprocal favors) is when resources seem most scarce and the economy is weakest. A non-zero-sum style of business is an acknowledgment that one's gain does not necessarily result in another's loss. Rather, many individuals and companies have found that their kindness and generosity bring them greater success, even when they may not expect it. Pooling resources, economies of scale, and creative collaborations show us how. The sum can be expanded by kindness so that the net result is greater wealth and success for both. One plus one *can* equal three.

No Good Deed?

The fragrance always stays in the hand that gives the rose.

—Hada Bejar, author

Occasionally the "no good deed goes unpunished" myth might *seem* to come true. In sports, as in business, we see some of the best and the worst of the human spirit. The 1964 bobsledding competition in the Winter Olympics provided a glimpse at true kindness of the sportsmanship variety. The Italian competitor Eugenio Monti had shown strongly in the final round of bobsledding. If the British team did not come through with a tremendous round, the Italian team was set to win the gold. For a moment, it looked like the British team was indeed out of the running, when British team leader Tony Nash discovered they had a faulty bolt on their bobsled and would have to withdraw. Seeing the dilemma, Monti gave the bolt from his own sled to Nash. The British team went on to win the gold medal, appearing to steal victory from the hands of the defeated Italian team.

In the immediate aftermath of the British team's win, Monti was scathingly attacked by his countrymen and the press. When criticized for having lost the gold medal, he reportedly said that "Nash didn't win because I gave him the bolt. He won because he had the fastest run." Monti was a true athlete and wanted to win a real match, not a race when his co-competitor had one hand tied behind his back. And Monti subscribed to the Olympic Creed: "[t]he most important thing in the Olympic Games is not to win but to take part, just as the most important thing in life is not the triumph but the struggle. The essential thing is not to have conquered but to have fought well."[6]

Monti's situation might seem to indicate that nice guys like him usually end up vilified and downtrodden, rather than taking home the gold. That is until you take the Power of Reciprocity into account. Monti's kindness did indeed come back to him. Monti is known as one of the most successful athletes in the history of bobsledding. His stellar record includes 10 World Champion medals and six Olympic medals. It was his sportsmanship— coming to the aid of a fellow competitor—that really made the headlines. He is best known and loved for his single act of kindness at the 1964 Olympics. Though he could not have seen it coming that fateful day, he did indeed have the full powers of reciprocity come to his benefit. Because of this good deed, he became the first athlete ever to receive the Pierre de Coubertin medal. This medal is sometimes felt to be an even greater reward than a gold medal and the International Olympic Committee considers it to be the highest honor. Monti became a household name for sportsmanship by being willing to put another's well-being ahead of his own. By his kind act and seemingly putting himself at risk, Monti was rewarded in ways he could not have imagined. So who was the real winner, after all?

Reciprocity likewise granted American mountain climber Dan Mazur a new career. When he gave up his own summit bid on Mt. Everest to rescue a climber from New Zealand who'd been left and presumed dead, Dan became an overnight sensation. Covered extensively in world press, including being called a "true American hero" on NBC's *Today Show*, his kindness has led him to a successful career lecturing and supporting the Mount Everest Foundation. Though his act of kindness caused him to forgo the summit, it gave Dan a new lease on life.

To avoid "playing the fool" even one time, you can and should be smart and savvy about your niceness. Kindness must be an empowering, gutsy choice. It takes courage, awareness, and judgment. Too much niceness might work against you, and become a barrier to your success. Let's look at ways to find balance and obtain all the benefits of niceness without getting tromped on: You'll want to avoid four pitfalls: smothering, ADDS, trying too hard to be liked, and excessive obliging. Yes, you can be *too* kind. In business, this can be a devastating mistake.

SMOTHERING

In your efforts to be nice, you can end up "smothering." You don't want to be like the parable of the butterfly mother. A butterfly mother watched anxiously as a baby butterfly tried to escape from its cocoon through the tiny opening at the top. The baby butterfly pushed at the tiny opening, gradually widening the opening, but at a certain point it stopped pushing and seemed overwhelmed. The butterfly mother desperately wanted to help and so she used her own legs to open the top of the cocoon. The baby butterfly then was able to come out of the cocoon without further struggle. But the happy union between mother and baby was thwarted. Although it was outside of the cocoon, its wings were too frail and underdeveloped to allow it to fly. Without strong wings developed from pushing its way out of the cocoon over several hours, it was doomed. As for the distraught butterfly mother, she had injured her own legs and now she too was in jeopardy.

Avoid excessive niceness. Too much of a good thing becomes, well, not a good thing anymore. Niceness must be taken with a dose of courage—to stand up for yourself, to strike a balance between being nice to others and taking care of yourself, and looking out for your own professional goals and aspirations. Your own well-being must, as a general rule, come first so that you have the strength and foundation to then take care of others and help them achieve their desires.

ADDS

By taking care of employees and others too much, they will not see the need to take care of themselves. You end up minimizing free will. The unassertive "too nice" boss will avoid giving realistic performance evaluations that would help the employee grow. The boss with ADDS—Assertiveness Deficit Disorder Syndrome—ends up doing a disservice to the employee.[7]

A boss with a dose of ADDS will sometimes shift these underperforming employees to other areas of the organization rather than disciplining or firing an employee. While it might seem nice, in the longer run the employee has no chance to learn, grow, and ultimately excel. Sheltered repeatedly from any failures, the employee does not learn to live up to the expectations and standards of the organization. The organization, too, is hurt as the employee continues to be a weak link in the other department.

TRYING TO BE LIKED

As a leader, it is counterproductive to pursue being liked by everyone, or trying to be just one of the team. Daniel Goleman, in his foundational work on leadership using emotional intelligence, warned against excessive use of "affiliative" leadership style. Reliance on affiliative, emotion-based leadership must be tempered with other strengths and strategies to avoid allowing feelings and emotions to take precedence over actually getting the job done. A senior vice president of a multibillion-dollar global company echoes Goleman's point: "We don't know how to be both kind and candid here....We're overly nice. Because we tend to shy away from confrontation, we don't give the kind of feedback that helps people grow."[8]

The inability to delegate can also hinder the too-nice boss who tries too much to be friends with staff, just one of the team. This can lead to doing instead of leading. As Lois Frankel points out in her books specifically designed to help women avoid the pitfalls of excessive niceness, helping others at the office can go too far: "If you're busy doing, you don't have time to provide the vision, guidance, technical support, and oversight required of a leader."[9] Delegating, providing direction, constructive feedback, and even criticism is part of, not contrary to, being a nice leader.

You should not be a whipping post for anyone. Especially when you take the first step to seed kindness in business, you do at times need to safeguard your niceness from being taken advantage of. At the office, you can work too hard and do too much for others to your own detriment. This happened to me several years ago. I had my head down and was working long hours to get the job done, assisting and crediting staff, and generally doing the "right" thing.

A person I supervised was strategically doing only the higher profile parts of her job, neglecting the more challenging, less visible aspects, and I ended up covering for her and making sure the job got done in order to satisfy our mutual boss. Although her output was significantly less than mine and also less than that of her coworkers, she made sure to be at the right meetings to represent *herself* well, and therefore seem to be a virtual expert in a number of important areas. I finally woke up to what was happening when people who mattered to my career were often greeting me with "How have you been? I haven't seen you in a long time!" I knew that my nose to the grindstone approach was being taken advantage of. When a face-to-face conversation with the staff member proved unsuccessful in coming to terms, I promptly pulled her off of the most high-profile meetings and reassigned her to other areas.

Can you guess what happened? When no longer able to "float" under my kindly cover, the staff person soon sought other work and, within a month, left the office in search of the next "too-nice" boss.

Excessive Obliging

Try practicing a healthy level of assertiveness in your personal life, too, so that you get accustomed to how it feels.

Remember that you are not obliged or required to do things with which you are uncomfortable. Kindness does not mean being nice because you feel bound by social constraints and whatever etiquette training you may have picked up along the way. Kindness is treating others with respect, honor, and care. Kindness is also treating yourself the same way.

Kindness does not extend to putting yourself in social, emotional, or professional jeopardy. While politeness is always critical, there is no need to engage in personal conversations or discussions with complete strangers, simply because you have accepted his or her offer of service. As a passenger in a taxi, it seems that many people feel compelled to have a lengthy conversation with the driver. I do not. Another common instance is the chatty airplane companion. When on an airplane, there are ways to handle your seatmate that are polite and yet close off conversation if you are not in the mood for it. You must use your own judgment, and while being sure to be polite, be extra sure to take care of yourself too.

If you receive bad service or a bad meal in a restaurant you should, albeit politely, comment on it, call the manager, or send the food back. If your friend wants to chitchat about something inconsequential for an hour when you want to spend time tending your garden, let him know that you have another obligation and will call him another time soon. If your boss expects you to come in every Saturday to clean up after the mess of your coworker, figure out a way to get your coworker to clean up his own mess or establish boundaries with your boss. You need free time too.

Being kind and courteous does not mean sacrificing your own comfort at every turn. Sometimes people will ask or expect you to give up things that you are not willing to in order to simply convenience themselves. On a plane in the summer of 2005, I was asked by a couple seated behind me to please switch

seats with them so that they could "stretch out." I was sitting in
what I considered the coveted exit row, on the aisle as I generally
prefer, with no one in the seat beside me. I had boarded the plane
in exhaustion and had gratefully sat down looking forward to
reading, maybe napping, and generally restoring my reserves in
preparation for the long week ahead. The couple was seated behind me, side by side, with another person by the window beside
them. If I said yes, I would then be in a row with less leg room
beside a stranger.

So I politely asked the requesting couple *why* they wanted to
switch, in an effort to see if perhaps there was a good reason that
I was simply not understanding at first blush. They were able-
bodied, middle-aged, and they were already seated together. They
had no reason, other than that they preferred my spot! If they
had had a small child with them, or an injury or disability that
made them uncomfortable where they were, I would have even
suggested the swap. If they were forced to sit apart, again I would
have gladly moved to facilitate their being together. But why
should I be expected to sacrifice my comfort for theirs? I, again
politely, declined, preferring to stay where I was. They did not
pursue it. A flash of guilt nagged at me and I spent several minutes going back over the exchange to be sure I had done the right
thing. *Did I?*

Smothering, ADDS, trying too hard to be liked, and excessive obliging—these are the primary faults that the too-nice

professional can fall into. If you suffer from any of these afflictions, becoming more aware of them helps. Recognize that you are benefiting no one by these actions, or inactions.

Genuine niceness in business is not the cookie-cutter saccharine-sweetness that reeks of insincerity as it is sometimes taught in customer-service training. Niceness does not even have to look and feel "sweet" to be genuine. When trusts and estates attorney Teresa Rhyne decided to part from a well-established Southern California business practice law firm and start her own law practice, she threw herself a grand opening party. I attended the local event, as did a couple hundred others. Teresa, known for her acerbic tone and often biting humor, was truly surprised at the number of people who came by to wish her well, bring her flowers, and generally support her new endeavor by choosing to attend her event. I told her in a congratulatory e-mail that it didn't surprise me in the slightest, because she has many friends and colleagues who like and respect her. Teresa, well aware of her frequently sarcastic style, asked, "Doesn't that kind of blow your whole 'kindness is key' theory?" I laughed and in my reply explained that there is not just one type of kindness—nice guys come in all shapes, sizes, and styles.

Rather, true niceness is both a sure pathway to individual success, and a remarkable community asset. Addison Walker had it right when he said that "It is not true that nice guys finish last. Nice guys are winners before the game even starts."

Practice Pointers

Remember there's no such thing as a small act of kindness. Every act creates a ripple with no logical end.

—Scott Adams, cartoonist and author

The Power of Reciprocity is the most ubiquitous of the kindness strategies. It can be expressed in many ways, from the seemingly mundane to the profound.

Simply pick someone to pay-it-forward to today. Don't restrict it to people in your professional circle, but instead seed kindnesses throughout your entire realm of influence and watch kindness capital grow. Try these techniques:

- Return phone calls, e-mails, and voice mails promptly.

- Keep your appointments and, if you have to cancel on short notice, call and follow up in writing with an apology.

- Make or pick up coffee for your coworkers and your employees from time to time.

- When you get your cup of coffee from the neighborhood cafe, pick one up for someone in another department, and drop it off with a smile at his or her desk.

- Pass on to a colleague a book you have enjoyed.

- Bring vegetables from your garden or a box of bagels to your office to share. Be sensitive to your coworker on a diet and don't plop a big box of donuts right by his or her desk.

- Donate items to the silent auction charity fundraiser that is organized by your firm.

- Take the time to show the ropes to the new person at work.

- Tell someone a compliment you overheard about them.

- Choose to be patient with a harried waitress, friendly with a stranger, or kind to a coworker.

- Leave a big tip for the waiter at the restaurant you frequent, and give your compliments to his boss.

- Let others speak and don't interrupt them.

- Think of your office place as an experiment zone and see if you can create a "glow of goodwill." Watch as it spreads.

- Don't let yourself fall into the trap of time-worn, but untrue, statements such as "nice guys finish last."

When you spread favors and kind acts in your professional life, you are rewarded with kindness capital for you and all the people you help. Add a positive personality and watch your kindness capital escalate.

Chapter 4

The Power of
Personality

Likeability may well be the deciding factor in every competition you'll ever enter.

—Tim Sanders, author, Yahoo! leadership coach

Oprah Winfrey's personal story is a lesson in many things: surviving, teaching, mentoring, and perseverance against odds. From poverty, abuse, and teen pregnancy, Oprah faced many obstacles. But more than anything else, her personal story is a lesson in the power of a positive outlook and a likeable personality. Oprah never backed down or allowed her negative circumstances to get in her way. Through it all, she chose to stay upbeat and believe in her ability to succeed.

Having made it past those barriers, Oprah has continued to give back throughout her incredibly successful career. Making generous charitable donations to worthy causes, she has bettered the situations of countless individuals. She has consciously initiated paying-it-forward by making cash gifts to audience members on her TV show and exhorting them to spread their abundance to others. Yet the most constant thing remarked about Oprah is that people like her. It is her positive, likeable personality, more than her guests or her causes, that draws people by the millions to her media outlets. Likeability has made her an icon.

Oprah certainly knows that kindness is a worthy goal in and of itself. She may not have thought that kindness and positiveness are also business assets.

From the company CEO to the coffeehouse barista, a *successful* professional is synonymous with a *likeable* professional. Likeability is, to be sure, an intangible quality hard to quantify and yet immediately recognizable.

When asked on the spot to name five likeable people, you don't struggle with the definition—the names pop right into your mind.

Likeable professionals share certain features. They are friendly, open, and charming. Most importantly, likeable professionals typically display a high quotient of positiveness. Positiveness, the antithesis to negativeness, is the easy-to-be-around, upbeat, and optimistic style that engenders good feelings in others.

Boosting your own level of likeability by being more positive is another potent, yet uncomplicated, way to develop kindness capital. You will want to choose positiveness and likeability when you realize that it is an immense favor to others. It makes them feel good. And it makes you feel good, too. These are the intangible benefits.

Then there are the tangible benefits of the Power of Personality. Throughout one's entire professional career—from getting your foot in the door, to rising to the highest posts in politics or the global economy—the power of a likeable personality makes a measurable difference. A likeable, positive personality will set you apart as you seek to establish your career or build your empire.

Conventional wisdom says that a leader must be respected to be successful. Hand-in-hand with respect, a leader must be liked.

Sure, we can all name a "cowboy" style, shoot-from-the-hip leader who has made it big. Donald Trump is one personality-centric businessperson and media personality who has flourished with showiness rather than likeability as a lead element of his success formula. But relying on a charismatic leader, whose strong and fiery personality makes headlines, is not usually the optimal business approach. In fact, company CEOs with charismatic personalities are more likely to lead a company to *failure* than success. Extensively examined by leadership expert and author Jim Collins in *Good to Great*, extreme personalities—characterized by big, high-profile style and panache—are typically *negatively* correlated with success.

Flamboyant, dominant leadership styles result in poor bottom-line performance for more than one reason. When the strong executive moves on, a weak company is often all that is left behind. This type of leader does not necessarily get the real facts but rather espouses what intimidated or awestruck employees want to hear. And an ego-induced reputation at the top sucks energy from the rest of the corporation, as the focus lies on leadership rather than results.[1]

The Power of Personality lies in a professional's ability to be, or become, likeable. The choice of becoming a likeable personality is yours to make: the key is positiveness.

Choose Cheer

We're hardwired to pick up each other's emotions—that's part of what allows us to communicate well.

—Dr. Thomas Sy, organizational psychologist

Think about a few of your more stressed-out colleagues. They do not need to snap or declare they are stressed for those around to recognize they are under pressure. The sound of their voice (clipped, strained?), how they stand (stiff, hunched in the shoulders?), and their overall presence (a "dark cloud" sensation?) tells you all you need to know.

We profoundly affect each others' moods, attitudes, and personal and professional outlooks. Thoughts and feelings are indeed intangible but incredibly potent. They radiate outward and are "readable" via attitude. What people are thinking and feeling can be understood from their body language, stance, facial expressions, voice intonation, and other cues.

Obviously your our own attitude is equally palpable to others, a real force that others can detect and feel. But, more importantly, attitudes are contagious.[2] A dark mood or negative attitude can put someone else on edge, make them irritated, or bring them down.

Therein lies an important part of the power of a positive personality. You have a tremendous tool to be kind and giving:

your positiveness. People automatically feel good in the presence of likeable, positive people; they feel good about themselves and their outlook on life improves.

Building kindness capital in your professional life is thus as simple as an attitude adjustment. Have a positive attitude as you go about your day. Interact positively with your customers, colleagues, bosses, and employees. Each person you encounter, even fleetingly, is uplifted by your positive presence. Think of it as a sort of "kindness energy" that you can cultivate in yourself, and allow to rub off on others.[3]

You might look at highly likeable people who seem positive all of the time and wonder how do they do it. Fortunately, likeability is not an endowed right for the fortunate few. Positiveness comes as much from free will as it does from nature. The current scientific consensus is that each of us has a sort of set-point for feeling good, but much of our positiveness, or conversely our negativity, is learned and therefore within our control to adjust. Positiveness is an acquired skill that is fluid and malleable, and one you can practice.

Knowing the immense impact we have on others, learning to project positiveness and likeability at every turn is truly a kindness imperative. "Cheerfulness is not simply an instinctive or spontaneous act of a person's nature but a conscious and courageous act of kindness. It's a gift one chooses to give to others," says ethicist and writer Michael Josephson.[4] It might mean that you consciously "cheer up" around a discouraged colleague, knowing that your mood will indeed rub off on him. Regardless of how you feel inside at any given moment, the attitude you choose to show to the world is up to you.

In addition to this "feel good" effect, a positive attitude sets up tangible benefits: the other part of the power of a positive personality. Professional success results from a positive, likeable personality in two quite distinct ways. First, an optimistic outlook creates an accomplishment mindset that manifests success like a self-fulfilling prophecy. Second, positive people are professionally popular—people *like* them. So they are chosen time and time again for professional opportunities.

Positive Plus

There is very little difference in people, but that little difference makes a big difference! The little difference is attitude. The big difference is whether it is positive or negative.

—William Clement Stone, businessman and
Nobel Peace Prize winner

Before Collette Lee, owner of Tower Realty in Southern California, gets out of bed in the morning, she consciously runs through the things she has to be positive about. A successful businesswoman and real estate broker, she coaches herself daily with a mantra she calls "Up Talk." Her morning pep talk to herself does not just count her blessings but also reaffirms her intent to go out of her way to be kind to everyone and to face any challenges with positiveness—an "I will not let anything get me down" attitude. Cultivating friends and acquaintances everywhere she goes, Collette's likeable, easy-to-be-around style draws people, and opportunities, to her. While other real estate companies have closed or suffered layoffs, Collette's niceness, positive attitude, as well as her extensive abilities in the Power of Connecting, carried Tower Realty through even the toughest real estate market downturn.

Cultivating a positive attitude is an incredible stimulator for your psychological well-being. When you choose to be positive—even if you temporarily "put-on" cheerfulness to help another feel good—you will also feel more positive as a result. And having a likeable positive attitude is a major professional asset—just ask Collette. Ultimately, achieving success largely depends on what you *think* your chances for success are.

The scientific and academic communities have laid the groundwork for professionals to recognize the importance of positiveness in achieving success. "Positive psychology," an approach that studies optimal human functioning, what is *right* with people, has taken off since the 1990s: Harvard University's class on positive psychology is among their most popular elective courses.

Optimists are quantifiably more successful than pessimists. When Dr. Martin Seligman, director of the Positive Psychology Center of the University of Pennsylvania, surveyed representatives of a major life insurance company, he found that those who expected to succeed sold 37 percent more insurance than those who were more pessimistic. The fact that pessimists are indeed more realistic (in other words, they see the world more accurately) than optimists should not mislead you into believing that optimists' rose-colored glasses lead them astray. Rather, optimists are *more* successful, even when they are less accurate in their interpretations of why negative things happen, because they choose to be positive and strive. Dr. Seligman found that optimists' sales records even got better and better as time went by, because their optimism produced persistence: "Optimistic individuals produce more, particularly under pressure, than do pessimists."[5]

Dr. Carol Dweck, Stanford University professor and author, similarly found that if you believe your lot in life is fixed then you will be unlikely to take chances or to learn new skills. Her study of junior high school students revealed that children who were taught to believe that their brains are like muscles (*keep building and exercising your brain and do not get discouraged*) correspondingly did significantly better in math than their peers.[6] The lesson: when you approach opportunities and hurdles positively, believing that hard work and learning will bring results, you do your utmost…and, accordingly, achieve the utmost.

Other studies have shown that feeling positive is a sort of cognitive lubricant. People work at their best when they feel good. Feeling good improves mental and performance capacity. Memory, decision making, learning, creativity, problem solving, and flexibility in thinking all are improved when you feel positive.[7]

The results for optimists include better paying jobs and more successful careers. College students have been tracked by Dr. Diener, professor of psychology at the University of Illinois, also known as "Dr. Happiness," to assess how financial success is linked to happiness, and positiveness. His widely reported study found that the positive, cheerful students became positive, successful adults, earning $25,000 more per year than their less positive colleagues.[8]

Tom Rath and Dr. Donald Clifton's research, which is examined in *How Full is Your Bucket?*, shows that being positive even makes *others* perform better. Not only do 99 percent of people want to be around more positive people but "...9 out of 10 report being more productive when they're around positive people."[9] Other supportive research they cite shows that workgroups where people are more positive than negative are significantly more productive than comparable, but negative, workgroups. Ratios of five positive interactions for every one negative were found to be ideal.[10]

Such results lead me to agree with Dr. Martin Seligman that: "An organization filled with optimistic individuals—or studded with optimistic individuals in the crucial niches—has an edge."[11]

Belief in self and others is a hallmark embraced by great leaders and successful people from every walk of life. But the business world still has a lot to learn from the study and practice of positiveness. Most companies have not yet adopted hiring techniques that assess attitudes and beliefs to augment standard interviews. Companies do not yet institute training programs to help their employees practice positiveness.

Are you taking the lessons of extensive research to heart, and attaining this edge? Are you consciously recruiting and hiring for a positive attitude? An analysis of your organization or workgroup may be in order to ensure that you are playing up the positive power of personality.

Although many businesses may not yet *consciously* recognize the effects of positive personalities on their businesses' bottom lines, they nonetheless *instinctively* gravitate toward positive, likeable business partners. The likeable person tends to be sought after in the professional world—to be on the best teams, in the high-powered offices, and as a preferred client. Want to get employees and coworkers to support you as you set the vision for your company? Hope that your boss will look favorably upon you during the next round of promotions? Aspire to political office? Or just wish your doctor would spend more time with you during your next office visit?

Think popularity.

Professional Popularity

It is your attitude, not your aptitude, that determines your altitude.
—Zig Ziglar, author and motivational speaker

Being likeable and making friends might initially sound out of place as professional goals. But when I coach people on professional accomplishment, I *always* recommend a personality self-assessment. People are surprised that a workplace *strategy* would need to account for *personality*. But, like it or not, popularity plays a big role in professional success. Some of the most reliable, hard-working professionals make the mistake of failing to nurture their connections and network at the office. Feeling that they are not at work to win a popularity contest, just there to get the job done, they are overlooked. The prime work groups, teams, and promotions go to people to whom others can relate, people they know—people they like.

How many whiny, bellyaching complainers do you choose to associate with in your professional life? Think of a project where you have the authority to assemble a team. You will be working together, perhaps traveling, and putting in long hours. Whom do you choose? Do you choose the vibrantly positive person who looks forward to the new project or the negative downer who is already punching holes in the plan? If you must choose between two suppliers, one who is competent but miserable to deal with and one who is both competent and charming, which one do you pick? (No question, right?)

Negative people are just not likeable.

Most businesspeople want to surround themselves with others who are strong positive influences. When you consider that most professionals spend about one-third of their lives working, it makes perfect sense that we would want to surround ourselves with positive people.

The "vacation test" should enter your mind when considering such choices: Is this person someone I would want to go on vacation with? Spend significant time with? Same goes for business partners, suppliers, and all of the professionals you rely on in your life from the plumber to the daycare worker. People will accept new clients, choose employees, and hire contractors largely on the basis of their likeability.

Likeable, positive people thus obtain jobs more easily. In highly social societies, so much of the assessment of the "fit" for a position depends on personality. Job skills can be readily taught and learned. Likeability though, is largely ethereal and therefore harder for companies to effectively identify and train for. Most customer-service training misses the mark by failing to identify personality components. Yet a likeable personality is truly essential for most professional positions. Of course, employees have to be competent to be hired, retained, and promoted. But given people of about equal qualifications, and having taken any affirmative action criteria into account, don't *you* choose who you simply like the best? Tim Sanders notes that "[Likeable people are] more likely to get second interviews, and more likely to get short-listed for jobs."[12] In fact, some research indicates that likeable people get more promotions and pay raises, period. *Even when they are less competent.*[13]

Having likeable, positive employees is an important way to respect and care for customers. According to Jack Mitchell, CEO of flourishing clothing stores Mitchells, Richards, and Marshs, the first criteria is hiring nice people. Mitchell is prepared to train for the technical skills needed to perform the task, but kindness is a prerequisite. Mitchell said, "We would absolutely never hire anyone who had fabulous skills who we didn't think fit our culture. If someone is a great person, he can usually acquire great skills through education. But in our experience, it's rare that someone with great skills can transform himself from a nasty to a nice person."[14] Without nice, likeable employees to engender loyalty, customers will continue to look for bargains and deals elsewhere.

Entry-level applicants need likeability to get them in the door, but leaders also benefit from exhibiting a positive personality.

Research conducted jointly by Yale University and the Center for Socialization and Development in Berlin in 2000 found that "the most successful leaders, from CEOs to PTA presidents, all treated their subordinates with respect and made genuine attempts to be liked. Their approach garnered support and led to greater success."[15] Likeable leaders model the way for their organization or workgroup by setting a positive tone...and know that the results follow.

One such positive leader, Konosuke Matsushita, knew that personality affects our ability to get people to gather around to give us support and bring us business. Founder of Matsushita Electric (the parent company of Panasonic) and the Matsushita Institute of Government and Management, his successful business career and management philosophy were the subject of a book called *Matsushita Leadership*. Matsushita was known as a gentle and friendly person with plenty of kindness capital. Attributing some of his extensive accomplishments to being amiable or likeable, Matsushita said, "What it comes down to is whether everybody loves you. If they think enough of you, they will go out of their way to buy your products. That is the way you have to work it; you have to be the kind of person and do the kind of work that people find irresistible."[16] When he died at age 94, he left a personal fortune of $3 billion and a company with $42 billion in revenues.

Advertising executives Linda Kaplan Thaler and Robin Koval in New York City understand a positive personality's link to business success too. Principals of one of the fastest-growing advertising agencies in the United States (with more than $1 billion in billings annually), they attribute its growth in a highly competitive field to "smiles and compliments" rather than cutthroat business practices in their terrific book, *The Power of Nice*.[17] Their positive, likeable persona is part of their business model, and they consciously cultivate kindness capital when they compete for clients and negotiate deals. Their financial success and exponential growth proves their own mantra: It pays to be likeable.

Observe how likeability works in politics. Early on, the favored Democratic nominee in the 2008 U.S. Presidential bid was Senator Hillary Clinton. Her credentials, experience, resources, and savvy positioned her as the presumptive winner in the early days of the campaign period. Until the likeability factor surfaced. People struggled to get to know her, to *like* her. Her personality was colloquially assessed as cool, unreachable, and not genuinely likeable. This intangible factor dogged Senator Clinton throughout the campaign, often overshadowing her qualifications and extensive knowledge. Charming and affable, Senator Barak Obama came from behind, picking up supporters at a stunning rate for reasons that were often not related to political strategy. People simply *liked* him better. He was more popular. He won the Democratic nomination.

Senator Obama's example was not an anomaly. Gallup Polls focusing on personality in presidential elections since 1960 show that one factor has been the best predictor of election victories—likeability.[18] More important than both the candidate's party affiliation and the actual policy issues, a likeable personality most closely correlates with winning. Just as people choose to do business with those they like, people vote for politicians they like.

At some level, it is indeed a popularity contest.

Works Like a Charm

You know nice when you see it, you know it when you feel it. If you don't see it or feel it, it's a good reason to pass.

—Jack Mitchell, author and clothing store CEO

Sure, politics and the public relations fields are affected by personality factors. But it does not matter much in other fields, right?

Wrong.

The legal field is thought of in many ways, but rarely in terms of likeability. Perhaps better known for rampant negativity, contentiousness, and overall unpleasantness, one could make the mistake of assuming that positive, likeable professionals and clients need not apply. But the legal profession too depends on likeability considerations in determining outcomes.

The personality of the individual plaintiff is strongly correlated to legal success. A court preparation trade publication carried an article by Dulin Kelly that made this point: "One item that keeps reappearing in cases tried or settled, is the likeability factor. If your client is a likeable person, this characteristic will, in all likelihood, affect the outcome of your case in two ways: First, the jury will want to award compensation to your client, because the jurors like him or her. This may overcome a case of close liability. Second, there is no question that if the jury likes your client the amount of compensation is likely to be higher."[19]

Fast-forward to the present day and you will see that the likeability factor is still strongly influencing legal outcomes. The highly respected law firm for which I worked in Vancouver, British Columbia, Canada, openly weighs the likeability factor in deciding strategy. When defending claims against a major client, the Insurance Corporation of British Columbia on motor vehicle accident cases, my former law firm Quinlan Abrioux evaluates the personality of the plaintiff (the person claiming injuries and requesting compensation) in assessing whether, and how, to litigate or settle the case.

After conducting a pre-court assessment of a plaintiff, senior partner Dennis Quinlan makes the first sentence of his written report to his client count. He sums up the plaintiff's personality. If they are genuine and likeable, he notes that they would make a "sympathetic witness"—one that a judge or jury would warm to. This is a red flag for his client, tipping them off that settling early or offering a higher payout would be an effective strategy. However, an unpleasant or disingenuous plaintiff means an "unsympathetic witness," and accordingly lays the way for negotiating harder and seeking a court date, safe in the knowledge that a judge or jury would not be swayed by any subconscious warm-and-fuzzy feelings toward the plaintiff.

A likeable personality not only helps you get where you want to be, but it also keeps you out of where you do not want to be. Like out of work. Economically challenging times, like the economic recession facing the United States in 2008, call for strategic boosting of likeability. When business is on the downswing, it is easier on management to dismiss less likeable employees: "People who are not liked by someone in authority are *always* the first to go when business conditions become unfavorable. It is not just enough to do a good job. Find ways to increase your likeability factors in the eyes of your employer," advises employment consultant James Challenger.[20]

This effect is not restricted to the realm of professional success. When people like you, they help you get what you want; they go out of their way for you. Leading with likeability, you get better service in restaurants, in doctor's offices, and in virtually all customer-service settings. This is because people *want* to help others who are nice, friendly, and charming.

The value of a likeable, positive personality includes making others feel good and making you more successful. With these benefits in mind, it is a good time to examine your own professional persona to ensure it is working effectively for you. As we examined earlier, fostering a positive outlook and banishing pessimism from your professional mind-set will help. But, in the meantime, image management techniques can instantly create and project likeability.

Image Matters

You must have this charm to reach the pinnacle. It is made of everything and of nothing, the striving will, the look, the walk, the proportions of the body, the sound of the voice, the ease of the gestures. It is not at all necessary to be handsome or to be pretty; all that is needful is charm.

—Sarah Bernhardt, French stage actress

Given all that is riding on it, you must take charge of your professional persona. But how do you ensure that your image includes a strong dose of that professional elixir, likeability? Start with the first impression.

The first impression is formed as you sit down with a business competitor to negotiate a merger, as you interview a potential employee, as you meet and greet clients at your firm's reception, or approach angel investors for startup funds. Do you know how much time it takes to make a first impression? When I teach image management, attendees are often surprised to realize that a mere 5 to 30 seconds is average.[21]

In this first crucial encounter, a number of very important judgments are made. In an involuntary, largely unconscious assessment process, we make a whole variety of instantaneous judgments about each other. Three absolutely crucial determinations are made about you.

> *Socioeconomic status.* This includes assessing how much money you make, your financial history, and even what side of the proverbial tracks you are from.

> *Educational attainment.* Are you well-educated or are you a high school dropout? Are you degreed or poorly educated? We all know that educational level is not an accurate indicator of true intelligence. And yet the close corollary, whether you are "smart" or not, is also part of this assessment.

Overall desirability. Are you a good candidate for the team, a good fit as boss or business partner? Are you someone who others want to spend time around?

Each of these three judgments must be positive in order to improve, or at least not hinder, your professional opportunities. First impressions are quite enduring, and hard to shake. The good news is that likeable, positive people are judged more positively on all three criteria. Let's see how your professional personality measures up.

Personality Self-Assessment

People buy personality as much as merchandise...
— Napoleon Hill, best-selling motivational author

What do you think a professional associate would say in describing you to a trusted colleague after first meeting? What three adjectives or descriptors would naturally pop into their minds? This is your current professional brand, like it or not.

In my courses on image management, I lead attendees through a series of analytical self-assessment exercises of this nature. Think of being spontaneously video-taped as you interact with others, such as at a business reception. Are you leading, in the first crucial seconds, with professionalism? Are you sure that you are wholly likeable? At this stage of self-assessment, honesty is particularly critical. It is important to become self-aware of your impression, to be as objective as possible.

The next step in creating your professional brand is to focus on how you would *like* to be perceived. How do you want others to see you? This should jibe squarely with who you really are at your core. As we have discussed, you must match what you portray to the world with who you really are in order to be seen as real and genuine. The art and science of image management is how to make your core strengths stand out and to minimize your less desirable traits.

If you had control over the three adjectives that pop into others' minds as they meet you, what three words would you ensure came rolling off their tongues in praise of you? These three adjectives form the core of your desired professional brand. This trinity becomes a mantra for the rest of my image management sessions.

People are often dissatisfied with what they believe their current image is. But I am always encouraged when they define their desired professional brand. Almost invariably, each participant in these image management sessions includes a likeability component as one of their top three choices. Factors such as open, positive, friendly, and kind are typically featured. People recognize the value of likeability in their professional image; they usually just have not previously put it into words.

For the corporation, this simple technique can cut through lengthy, complex programs and expensive marketing programs. Having a three-word corporate brand that leads with a likeability factor establishes a positive brand strategy and begins to build kindness capital.

Once aware of the value of personality factors in their professional brand, most are nevertheless uncertain of how to get there. The last exercise that I lead participants through in pursuit of a likeable, positive professional image is how to actualize this coveted brand. Image management shows you how to modify your image to create good first impressions and an enduringly likeable personality.

Branding and designing an image requires examination of the techniques that create more likeability, and other desired professional brands, including body language and posture; dress and appearance; facial expressions; written communications; presentation skills; as well as choice of words, enunciation, and vocal quality. Very subtle adjustments in stance, speaking style, and business etiquette results in dramatic changes in likeability levels. Without trying to cover a full course in image management in the space here, one technique will most effectively help your likeable positive personality come through—the smile.

Summon a Smile

If you are not using your smile, you're like a man with a million dollars in the bank and no checkbook.

—Les Giblin, award-winning
salesperson and best-selling author

I have had the opportunity to work with a variety of businesses and professionals, but none so interesting as law enforcement personnel. Sheriffs, police chiefs, and public safety administrators are generally not best known for their likeability or positiveness. Nevertheless, their public service mandate and individual professional goals usually include cultivating trust and creating open-door approachability that welcomes, rather than intimidates, the public that they serve.

My best advice to them, and to other professionals, always includes making ample use of the simple smile. The smile is the best and quickest way to easily create a positive, likeable persona.

Male law enforcement officers in particular benefit from adding a smile to their persona. A smile is the most powerful exhibitor of a positive personality. This "attitude flag" can make the difference between a positive public rating and a negative one. It sends a message of friendliness, connection, and lack of intent to do harm. In some ways, a smile is like the wag of a dog's tail. It is a way of indicating that we are nonthreatening and are interested in encountering others.

A smiling person scores higher when being assessed by others on first meeting. They appear more confident, successful, and approachable. Experience indicates that cutting to the chase and simply training staff to smile is often as effective as elaborate customer service and customer sensitivity skills training programs.

The smile is also the simplest, most immediate kindness of all. The smile serves both the smiler and the recipient of the smile in one of the most effective, easiest acts of kindness. The smile lights up not only the wearer's face and makes them feel good, but it also spreads positive emotion to others who see that expression and involuntarily react to it.[22] The smile is the most contagious of all emotional indicators, and it spreads easily and rapidly.[23] A smile from a customer-service representative means they acknowledge your right to be served. A smile from your boss means that she recognizes the good job you have done and that your overtime hours have not gone unappreciated. Your shareholder's warm smile and greeting tells you they are pleased with your performance.

With all the benefits of a positive, likeable personality, you would think that developing this personality type would be on the top of our professional improvement lists. But it, like the other Powers, is sometimes waylaid by naysayers and urban myth…and by the "me first" syndrome.

Kindness Inhibitor: *The "Me First" Syndrome*

The Golden Rule is of no use whatsoever unless you realize that it is your move.

—Dr. Frank Crane, minister and columnist

We are busier than ever, and it shows. People force their way onto the freeway without so much as a wave, people stride by without a word while others hold the door, workers toil away tirelessly without a simple acknowledgment, and it can be many moons before a thank-you note ever graces your mailbox. (No, not your e-mail inbox—your *actual* mailbox.)

We are also ruder than ever, and that shows too. Studies throughout the early 2000s show a slippage in civility, and a steady decline. One poll showed that this slippage is quite rapid: nearly 70 percent of those surveyed in the United States believe that our society was less civil than it was the previous year. [24]

Less sleep, more stress, more traffic, fewer limits, and lessened expectations are the hallmarks of today's society. Isolation and anonymity are common byproducts of personal technologies, solitary work habits, and declining community involvement in what is sometimes called the "me-first and me-only" era. The modern day has ushered in advances and innovations—and created many contradictions. Gen Y and Gen X, while laying claim to a strong sense of environmentalism, personal liberties, and respect for diversity, have all but let common courtesy go by the wayside. Failure to attend to those around us—largely ignorant of how much we affect, and are affected by, others in our personal and professional lives—is leading to a declining stock of kindness capital in our society.

Take your pick of where to lay the blame for the decline in courtesy and reduced capacity to connect. We live in exceedingly close quarters to each other. The population density of our urban cities is increasing as more people choose to live in cities rather than suburbs or rural areas. Media influences bombard us daily, making swearing and rudeness seem *de rigueur* and even "cool." Parents struggling to keep up with the fast pace of modern life seem to be letting the instruction of common courtesy fall by the wayside. This downward trend is startling, given the real benefits of kindness capital in our personal and professional lives.

Courtesy (often thought of as good manners, politeness, etiquette, and civility) builds kindness capital. Courtesy captures the essence of showing consideration for the feelings and rights of others, and is anything but superficial. Courtesy lowers the tension in our lives and reduces the stress that we face. It is the oil that greases the mechanisms of our daily social and professional lives, making things more comfortable and pleasant for all of us.

Several years ago a coworker, Troy Brown, took a heavy box out of my hand as we walked into our building at the same time. He held the box on the elevator ride up, and he carried it to my desk and put it there for me. I was pleased, and surprised. But shouldn't I reasonably expect a stronger person, carrying less, to do that out of courtesy and kindness?

Sadly, kind acts such as Troy's are a rarity these days. Too often tied up in gender and racial implications, a man offering to carry something for a woman could be perceived as implying that he is more able than she. A black person holding the office door for a white person could be perceived as a statement of subservience or inequality. Many of these considerations hamper individuals from making these simple, yet meaningful, statements of kindness, courtesy, and ultimately respect for another human being.

There is a reason that the Troy Brown incident years ago still stands out in my mind: it has not happened again.

But kindness capital in the form of common courtesy is truly an imperative, and must be adhered to if we are to live together in cities and towns, buy each others' products, work together, and raise the next generation together. There is a common good that exists in any organized society. What's more, the health of business and our economy requires bucking the "me-first" syndrome with the building of kindness capital. Niceness is not a windowdressing; it is a necessity.

Niceness Is a Necessity

Virtue is a social necessity.

—Michael Josephson, ethicist and author

A quaint, yet insightful, anonymous parable illustrates how closely intertwined we are, both personally and professionally, with all of our neighbors:

There was a farmer who was the premier corn grower in his community. His corn was always sweeter and better than anyone else's, and it always won the blue ribbon at the county fair. At the end of the growing season, he would take his seed corn, the corn that would be sown the following spring, and gave a large portion of it to all the farmers in the area. "Why do you do that?" someone asked him. "Don't you want to keep the best corn for yourself?"

"I do it for myself," replied the farmer. "My corn will be cross-pollinated by bees and wind from the other fields, and if they have inferior corn, mine will soon become inferior as well."

Now try to imagine a society where we all ignored our interconnectedness and choose to "do our own thing" to the exclusion of others. There would be no reason to follow traffic rules, say please or thank you, or really even stay within the boundaries of the law. The consequences would be profound. Michael Josephson asks us to think about the rule of universality in making choices: "Do only those acts which you are willing to allow to become universal standards of behavior applicable to all people in similar situations. Ask yourself: If everyone did it, would it be a good thing?"

Everyday experiences, such as grocery shopping, would be transformed into hazardous experiences. An old friend of mine shared a story about a shopping trip to a congested, crowded Costco store. Pam saw a me-first attitude being exhibited by many shoppers: carts were bumped, people were cut in front of, and lines were jumped. Pam, however, continued to excuse herself, say "sorry" when her cart was bumped by another, and wait her turn to access the sale stacks.

After leaving the store, Pam's husband vented about the frustration and overall unpleasantness of the shopping trip. Why, he asked her, did she continue to be so polite and easygoing, when literally no one responded in kind? Pam explained that it was the right thing to do and reflected on how she had been raised by her parents to practice courtesy. But, more importantly, she felt strongly that she *must* continue to be civil. Her smile, "excuse me," or generous behavior, was necessary to both counteract bad behavior and to act as an example to others.

Everyone wants to get the best products (choicest produce, best cut of beef), get the best value (sale items, freshest products), and get the shopping done as quickly as possible. Without Pam (and people like her) practicing courtesy in balancing others' interests with their own, social order would become strained.

One very widely adhered to and unstated rule in social interactions is that one does not come into physical contact with another person. The North American standard is a 2- to 4-foot personal space distance, with a comfort zone for casual social or public interactions being 4- to 10-feet or more. Now imagine that the constraint against touching and contact was ignored by everyone in their anxiousness to meet their shopping goals. Tempers would flare as each person saw the other as an obstacle to their goals. In the extreme, aggressively bumping others' carts out of the way would not be unrealistic. With civility by the wayside, there would be chaos at Costco. In order to maintain a civil setting, people like Pam *have* to be courteous—in shops, in businesses, and on the roads.

Be Nice to Your Neighbor

It's hard for a fellow to keep a chip on his shoulder if you allow him to take a bow.

—Billy Rose, Broadway producer
and theater/nightclub owner

As tempers flare and incidences of road rage continue to rise, niceness is, indeed, a necessity on our freeways. Without courtesy, our freeways and roadways would potentially become impassable.

Road rage is blamed on many factors that are really mere excuses. Most blame long commutes, traffic congestion, tight schedules, and stress for the increasingly common incidents of threats, assault, and violence we see on the highways. But the real reason that road rage exists is not found in these time-worn excuses. Road rage results from feeling disrespected and disconnected, a phenomenon of increasing potency in our modern society.

To be seen, heard, and understood—to be respected—is a basic human need. This concept underpins the Power of Thanks and the Power of Connecting. The feeling of being "flipped off" causes the ego of a frustrated driver to flare. The need to be respected rises to the surface, and road rage is the result. When you seem to drive too slowly, drive too fast, drive in the wrong lane, or inadvertently cut off someone in this frame of mind, the perceived insult is like salt in a wound. It is not surprising that in today's parlance a harsh insult is considered a "diss"—disrespectful.

We are advised to protect ourselves from road rage by keeping our doors locked, following the rules of traffic, and staying alert to erratic behavior on the road. But this misses the point of actually preventing and ultimately reversing road rage. Studies have shown that more than 85 percent of road rage incidents would be defused by an apology. The only way to contribute to that solution is to retaliate with courtesy and respect.

Aggressive driving, the milder cousin to road rage, is so common that it is largely accepted. Acts of aggressive driving, such as tailgating, driving on the shoulder of the road, or cutting people off, is anything but courteous in spite of its relative acceptance. Have you ever impatiently and thoughtlessly tailgated another car, only to have it pull into the house right next door to yours? That wash of embarrassment you felt tells you that such driving is not kind.

Road rage feeds on the prevalent feelings of disconnection and lack of societal connection. When we do not know the nameless and faceless person zooming by on the freeway, and they do not know us, there seems to be no consequence to being rude. Ever wondered what would happen if we all treated the person driving in the car next to us like our neighbor? Or imagined that everyone who is sharing the road is a friend, a coworker, or a relative? When familiar with the person in the other car, aren't we less inclined to speed up behind them, slam on the brakes, and honk when they take an extra second to accelerate at a stop sign?

You can be that example—the courteous "Pam"—who bucks the road stress trend. There is nothing to prevent you from easing back and letting another car in front of you when merging onto the freeway. Intentionally being kind even when it does not immediately benefit you, and in fact puts you one car back in the line of traffic, is a smart thing to do. If you don't let that car in and instead hold firmly on to your spot, what happens to that person? In theory, if everyone refused to ease back, that car trying to merge on to the freeway would literally never get on. Or, even worse, that person trying to merge on could get fed up and force themselves on to the road, potentially causing an accident. What an absurd result! Thank goodness we as individuals can choose to be the one to let them on. Although we have the "right" to drive on the freeway, that privilege is tempered by the rights of others: "Your right to swing your arm ends at the tip of my nose," says Michael Josephson.

When someone shows you the courtesy of letting you in line, it is your chance to show your appreciation. In all but the worst neighborhoods, it is an understood gesture of thanks to wave your hand briefly and smile as you are let in. I often see people respond with their own smile when they see "thanks" written on my face.

It can be a challenge to consciously practice courtesy in our daily lives, especially behind the wheel. It takes even more strength to display courtesy to others who are not courteous in response or who may be downright rude. But to reverse the startling trend toward increasing roadside aggression, you and I must take the high road. We can each help to drive a new culture of courtesy on the road ahead. The person in the car next to you really is your neighbor.

One way to contribute to this change is to act on your good intentions.

Actualize Intentions

The smallest act of kindness is worth more than the grandest intention.
—H. Jackson Brown, best-selling author

We, quite naturally, judge ourselves by our intentions. We know that we intend to write that thank-you note, that we truly mean to help our coworker with his project, that we expect to find the time to take a new colleague out for coffee, that we tried to bring a casserole to a sick neighbor. But unless our intentions—what we plan to do—are translated into what we actually do, they matter little.

Because we *intend*, we sometimes don't *do*. Have you ever thought to yourself: "I just got too busy this time, but next time for sure I'll do it," and then just moved on without concern? Michael Josephson illustrates it this way: "Five birds are sitting on a telephone wire. Two of them decide to fly south. How many are left? Three, you say? No, it's five. You see, deciding to fly south is not the same as doing it. If a bird really wants to go somewhere, it's got to point itself in the right direction, jump off the wire, and flap its wings."

We are judged by what we actually do. Your loved ones, your boss, and the people you do business with do not benefit from what you planned or intended to do. If you intended to call your friend that you had lost touch with, but did not make that call, does the fact that they were on your mind matter? Certainly not to them. Or if you thought of writing a note to a store manager commenting on the great service you received, your lofty intent does not make an iota of difference to the career or self-worth of that staff person. Renowned social writer Eric Hoffer challenges us to see if our good intentions are matched by our actual deeds: "If you were arrested for kindness, would there be enough to convict you?"

The biggest barrier to taking action is "waiting for the right time." We hesitate, we wait, we postpone. We don't want to act unless we are "ready"—the fruitless pursuit of the best use of time and energy is a typical "Type A" personality pitfall. We put off writing that thank-you note until we can buy new note paper or matching stamps, or we seek out the perfect quote or the inspiration to express ourselves profoundly. When we unearth the reminder much later and realize the opportunity has passed, we shrug our shoulders and promise that we'll make it up—at the right time.

Riverside, California Mayor Ron Loveridge has often said that City Hall should "satisfy not maximize." Better to get the project underway, the pothole filled, or a few trees planted than to put them off in favor of developing an infallible plan, repaving the whole street, or landscaping the entire park. Sometimes grand intentions fail to materialize into concrete, executable plans. When bogged down in details, costs, or politics, something is better than nothing. Break larger projects into smaller increments. If a few shade trees go into the park, and the park is thus more useful to the neighboring residents, the chances of gaining support for a major landscape augmentation in the future is that much more likely anyway. Mayor Loveridge knows that intentions often stand in the way of accomplishments.

Yep, something is better than nothing. And late is better than never. I sent a thank-you note to a colleague who had done a good turn for me—two months after the fact, I hate to admit. This was clearly a breach of proper etiquette, as two weeks is the limit for such niceties. However, when I received his grateful phone call acknowledging my note, I knew I had done the right thing by turning my intention into action, even if it was delayed action. If you want to do something for your sick neighbor, skip the grand plan for the home-cooked three-course meal that will never squeeze into your busy schedule. Instead, pick up something extra at your favorite Chinese takeout when you order dinner for your family. If you have the time, pop a ribbon on the bag and even spend a few minutes visiting when you deliver your gift, and actually *do* the favor you wanted to do. You will be amazed at how these little things add up, both personally and professionally.

Mere forgetfulness can also get in the way of actualizing good intentions. Planning and scheduling intentional acts of kindness on your day-timer, to-do list, PDA, or even a sticky note is a way to make it a real commitment—the more likely you will follow through on your intentions. And yet few of us take that simple step of committing ourselves in writing. Why is it that we have no difficulty packing our schedules full of appointments, meetings, and obligations that are tangibly work-related, but find it hard to set aside the needed time for demonstrating care for others?

Much like scheduling time for exercise, time for fun, or time to read your favorite book, setting aside time to turn good thoughts into kind acts seems somehow much harder than documenting a meeting or project deadline. Our culture of haste, combined with our bottom-line society, tells us that only those things that lead to accomplishments "count." We accordingly only write down those things we think will lead to concrete achievements, letting relationship- and reputation-building activities go undocumented and often undone.

Without action, intentions go nowhere. An anonymous writer said it best: "Remember, people will judge you by your actions, not your intentions. You may have a heart of gold—but so does a hard-boiled egg."

Practice Pointers

If the world seems cold, then ask yourself, "How many fires have I kindled today and how many have I doused?"

—Harvey Hornstein, social scientist and author

It is not difficult to become more likeable and positive. The Power of Personality can be expressed in a myriad of everyday activities:

- Ask the opinions of all the stakeholders with whom you interact. Even if you don't use their advice, they will appreciate that you respected them enough to ask.

- Use people's names. People feel good when they hear their name.

- Be friendly. Make a point to meet new people and introduce them around your place of work.

- List those with whom you work who are primarily positive and are largely negative. If you are in a position of authority, think of whether you need to make any changes in your work environment to ensure that positiveness is the predominant flavor of your milieu.

- Support your staff publicly.

- Consult staff before changing their responsibilities so that they feel part of the decision.

- ❧ Conduct your own professional brand assessment. Assess, honestly, whether you need to increase your likeability.

- ❧ Put visual reminders (something as simple as decorative sticky notes will suffice) around your home and office to remember to be grateful/ thank someone/be positive, and so on.

- ❧ Make ample use of the smile throughout your day.

- ❧ Think of yourself as your business's CKO (Chief Kindness Officer) and see what duties you can assign yourself.

- ❧ Use your PDA to set reminders throughout the day to prompt you to do something for someone else. It could simply remind you to look up and smile.

- ❧ Revise your hiring practices to more accurately assess candidates' personalities.

Likeability, as with all of the Powers, has a tremendous two-way street effect: bringing good feelings to all you encounter and good results to you and your business. Thanking is also a quick and easy way to create incredible levels of kindness capital.

Chapter 5

The Power of Thanks

The deepest principle in human nature is the craving to be appreciated.
—William James, Harvard professor of
psychology and philosophy

Ding! went the Compliment Machine: "People are drawn to your positive energy." Ding! "You are always there when needed." With just a small sign identifying the "Compliment Machine" on 14th Street NW in Washington, D.C., the random compliments that issued from this unusual machine kept coming in a steady stream punctuated by drawn out pauses. The brain child of visual artist Tom Greaves, displayed in 2007 in conjunction with a collection of public art in the area, the Compliment Machine delivered general positive phrases of appreciation—simple compliments—all day long as onlookers hustled by. Ding! "You leave things better than you find them." It was hoped that these random words of appreciation might actually spur anonymous passersby to feel better, and perhaps even do better.

It just might have.

Thanking and appreciation, you see, has the power to inspire and motivate, to influence, to increase productivity, and even to change lives. What a profound way to demonstrate kindness! If you have ever passed up an opportunity to thank someone in business and then shrugged it off thinking "*it wouldn't have mattered anyway,*" think again.

Dramatic stories abound. Average employees with self-esteem problems have achieved the highest ranks of corporate America after a well-placed word of encouragement. High-tech millionaires were once kids on the wrong side of the tracks until an appreciative elder acknowledged their worth.

Thanks can be the turning point in a business deal. Stephen M.R. Covey shares the story of real estate agent Tom Peek in his book *The Speed of Trust*. Tom Peek was one of several top Realtors invited to make a pitch to represent the developer of an exclusive parcel of land in Park City, Utah. The land was expected to be developed and become very profitable, so the competition was stiff. Tom made his presentation, which was on par with that of the other top Realtors. At this point, the decision of the developer was difficult, trying to differentiate one well-qualified real estate agent from the other. Tom made it easy for them both by distinguishing himself using the Power of Thanks. He was the only bidder to send a handwritten thank-you note to the developer. He got the deal. And, yes, the developer credited the thank-you note as the decisive factor in tipping his decision in favor of Tom. The value of Tom's thank-you was enormous: the development, The Colony, became the largest ski-in and ski-out homesite development in North America, and Park City became one of the 2002 Winter Olympics sites.[1] You can do the math on that one.

Less dramatically—but by no means less importantly—people are encouraged and motivated every day by a thoughtful show of appreciation. When you harness the Power of Thanks in your professional life, you will see the self-esteem, confidence, and well-being of those around you shoot up. All stakeholders—customers, suppliers, employees, coworkers, and shareholders—thrive on being appreciated.

If you have a strong sense of security and assuredness of your own self-worth, congratulations. You are one in a million. If you are like the rest of us, you crave, literally require, regular reassurance and reinforcement of your personal and professional value. Am I good enough? Do I have what it takes? "All of us are self-centered, suckers for a bit of praise, and, generally, like to think of ourselves as winners," said Thomas Peters and Robert Waterman in their influential examination of what motivates the leaders of top-performing American companies.[2] Everyone, from the line worker to the most successful entrepreneur or political leader, feels insecure and unrecognized on occasion, and often at the deep core level.

This plague of insecurity is the greatest threat to our well-being, the cause of much discord and conflict. When uncertain about our worth—as humans or as professionals—we tend to look for the worst in others, in our business forecasts, in our outlook on life. When doubting our own intrinsic value, we rush, make bad decisions, and let our egos rule. We even perpetuate or instigate conflict to try to artificially create a sense of security or control: "Half of the harm that is done in this world is due to people who want to feel important....They do not mean to do harm....They are absorbed in the endless struggle to think well of themselves," said T.S. Eliot.

It is no surprise, then, that acknowledging and thanking is such a great kindness...and has such profound effects. Thanking creates immense kindness capital, in two related ways. First, top-notch employees drawn to businesses with caring reputations will stay, and thrive, when they are appreciated and made to feel good about themselves. Second, thanking boosts productivity and performance: making employees and other stakeholders feel important (like winners) gains their loyalty, their best efforts, and their business.

Thriving on Thanks

Praise does not cost anything to give, but its benefits on employee morale are priceless.

—Michal Ann Strahilevitz, marketing professor

Having a reputation for caring draws the best in the business to your ranks, whether you have a multinational software company or a small independent print shop. Once you have attracted stellar employees, persuading them to stick around and invest their best efforts is the next order of business. Ample use of thanking and appreciation allows you to grow the positive work environment that underpins a solid stable of staff and colleagues.

After years of focus on assembly-line efficiency and business process re-engineering, many 21st-century businesses are wakening to the realization that people truly are their main asset. Top technology, patents, ideas, financial resources, and equipment all have a crucial role in professional success. But without talented and motivated people to design, create, and operate them, even the most cutting-edge business plan cannot be executed. Ample natural resources, best machinery, and extensive real estate holdings cannot make up for an implementation team that is deficient in kindness capital.

Virtually all businesses pay lip service to taking care of their people, but savvy companies actually prove their commitment by investing in kindness capital. Companies known for keeping the best and brightest engaged offer their employees evidence of that commitment: training, opportunities for advancement, a fun environment, a sense of purpose or valuable mission (as we'll look at in Chapter 6)…and frequent and sincere appreciation for their hard work.

Ample and sincere thanking is the most direct and straightforward way to engage and encourage employees. Employees consistently rank receiving thanks at the top of their reasons for enjoying work and staying at a particular company. One-third of CFOs and workers responding to a Robert Half International survey said frequent recognition is the most effective form of motivation.[3]

Southwest Airlines knows this. When a businessman accidentally left his wallet on a Southwest airplane, a caring employee wound his way through the crowds, following him all the way to his car to hand the wallet over to him. Delighted, this frequent traveler recognized extraordinary service and kindness and, so, wrote a letter to the company commending the employee. A couple of weeks later, the CEO of Southwest wrote a letter to the employee enclosing the traveler's letter and adding his own praise and appreciation. For a CEO to take the time to pass on a letter of thanks and to write his own to an employee greatly boosted the employee, and doubly impressed the traveler who told me all about it.

The best and brightest employees will not stay where they are not appreciated; they will seek out environments with flourishing kindness capital. Failing to thank and perpetuating or allowing an unkind environment to flourish is a guaranteed way to lose business, revenue, friends, colleagues…and employees.

Thank Your Way Through the HR Treadmill

Brains are like hearts—they go where they are appreciated.
—Robert McNamara, former U.S. Secretary of Defense

Failing to thank sets up a nasty cycle—constantly losing employees, refilling positions, and dealing with the negative undertow of unengaged employees. Thousands of dollars spent in retraining, lost time, and lawsuits result from high employee turnover.

Many an entrepreneur has been born out of frustration, trying to escape from a negative boss or hostile, unappreciative work
environment. Job satisfaction is much more the result of one's
relationship with the boss than the amount of money earned. A
Gallup poll survey of 2 million employees at 700 American companies "…found that what determines how long employees stay—
and how productive they are—is the quality of their relationship
with their immediate boss." The survey, finding that people are
four times more likely to leave a job when they have a boss who
doesn't appreciate them as when they have a supportive one, proved
Marcus Buckingham's observation that "People join companies
and leave managers."[4] In fact, the number one reason that most
Americans quit their jobs is due to feeling unappreciated.

In case you are tempted to breeze through, thinking that your
business is pretty well off (*no lawsuits pending, no noticeable grum-
bling in the ranks*), take note of the enormous scale of this problem and take another look. Tom Rath and Donald Clifton
estimate in their best-selling book *How Full Is Your Bucket?* that
there are upwards of 22 million workers in the United States
who are "actively disengaged"—a state of apathy brought about
by not being acknowledged.[5] Engaged employees, those committed to their companies' success and willing to go the extra
mile, are estimated at just 14 to 21 percent of the workforce
worldwide.[6]

This leaves a rather large segment of workers who are not
totally disengaged but are certainly nowhere near top performing.[7] These unappreciated, unengaged employees pull back on

their efforts, have higher absentism, perform more poorly, and have higher injury rates, ironically making it less and less likely they will get the appreciation they want.

One negative employee can contaminate the pot for others, dragging down overall workplace morale and productivity. Employees often feel quite disturbed by others' failure to be kind and considerate. In one survey, workers reported on their reaction to unkindness and incivility in the workplace. The results showed that 63 percent felt less organizational commitment, and 37 percent admitted decreasing the effort they put into their work. Shockingly, 70 percent contemplated changing jobs. And 9 percent lost work time by calling in sick.[8]

The price paid in organizations for disengaged, dissatisfied employees directly affects the bottom line. Rath and Clifton's 2004 estimates put the impact of associated lost productivity, injury, illness, absences, and fraud at $1 trillion per year in the United States.[9] Ouch!

Thanking can counteract these negative outcomes, causing people to work harder and accomplish more. Employees that are thanked and recognized for their efforts will feel like winners...and *perform* like winners.

Like a Winner

Everyone has an invisible sign hanging from his neck saying, "Make me feel important!" Never forget this message when working with people.

—Mary Kay Ash

When Mary Kay Ash, entrepreneur and founder of Mary Kay Cosmetics Inc., pointed out the invisible placard we all carry around, she acknowledged the deep-seated desire of all individuals—to be made to feel important and recognized, to *feel* successful.

Mary Kay Ash operated her immensely successful business venture on the basis of the golden rule, developing her company to more than $2 billion in annual retail sales at the time of her death in 2001. Ash's marketing plan was designed to facilitate her female employees' success in the company. Known for enthusiastic support and praising of her employees, she coined the phrase "praising people to success." Ash knew that the most effective way to make people feel like winners, and perform like winners, is to simply thank them and acknowledge their contributions. "I believe in the personal touch, because it makes every human being feel appreciated," Mary Kay said in her autobiography.[10]

Yep, "nothing succeeds like success." People not only feel good when they are treated like winners, they actually become more successful. In one study, adults were timed to see how well they did in solving 10 puzzles. Regardless of the actual results, half of the adults were told they did rather well, with seven of 10 right answers. The other half of the subjects were told they did poorly, with only three correct answers. When another set of puzzles was then given to the subjects, the ones who thought they had succeeded the first time around actually did well on the second round when their real results were tallied. The poor saps whose self-esteem was shot down by being told they'd scored poorly the first round, *did* do poorly on the second set of puzzles.[11] People live up to your expectations, be they of success—or of failure. If you "label a man a loser...he'll start acting like one."[12] Conversely, the glow of being recognized for their (purported) success seemed to have driven the subjects on to achieve more.

Treating team members like successes invariably creates a more positive, and mutually helpful, work environment for all. In another psychological study, a test was given to male and female school teachers. Some of the teachers were told afterward that they did well on the test, while others were told that they did not do well. Immediately after being either complimented for a job well-done, or told they had done poorly, the teachers witnessed an overburdened young woman trying to balance far too many items. When she inevitably dropped some of the items, the teachers who had been treated like winners by being told they had succeeded on the test were three times more likely to help her than their discouraged counterparts.[13] Feeling successful made the teachers more likely to help another out and thus spread a glow of goodwill. Imagine the benefits in your workplace if all team members *really* acted like a team? Positive reinforcement can help create this effect.

Positive Reinforcement

Recognition is the greatest motivator.

—Gerald Eakedale

Some of the most successful businesses in the world make sure their employees feel like winners by actively facilitating them doing things right, even if they have to create the circumstances to make it happen. IBM sets its sales quotas relatively lower than some of its competitors, so that about 70 to 80 percent of its salespeople actually succeed in meeting the quotas. The "successful" salespeople are bolstered to strive to meet and exceed their own records, shooting up sales for the company. In *The Heart of a Leader*, Ken Blanchard recommends an active strategy to make your people feel good about themselves, suggesting that leaders should actively set out to "catch" people doing things right by simply dropping in on operations and walking around noticing positive efforts.

Thanking reinforces a job well-done, and encourages people to work hard to be worthy of thanks in the future. Classically known as positive reinforcement, when you thank people for doing something well, they feel good about it and consequently learn to do it again. When you thank a supplier for meeting your deadline or delivering your product early, they replicate that behavior (and feel good about themselves and about you).

Studies have also indicated a scientific reason for why praise works so effectively. Receiving praise triggers the same area of the brain (the reward center) as does receiving money.[14] The recipient of praise and acknowledgment simply feels good. Naturally, that person is motivated to do more of whatever got him the praise. Praising employees reinforces and motivates high performance and guarantees they will try hard to be worthy of your thanks in the future.

Most employees, within proper parameters, not only meet your positive expectations, but exceed them. Giving them an environment conducive to bringing out their best is not only good for them, but the smart way to develop your staff. Employees will work harder for someone they respect and trust to care about them. Employees, suppliers, and contractors will all "go the extra mile" when they know you are interested in their outcomes, their best interests, too. They will move your order to the top of the pile, work late, and even bend a rule or two for you if they know that you trust them and are counting on them.

Tom Raft and Donald Clifton's analysis of more than 10,000 business units in 30 industries revealed amazing results from thanking. Rath and Clifton created a metaphor of filling or emptying each others "buckets." Like drops of water into a bucket, we can make others feel like winners by filling their metaphorical buckets with positive reinforcement through compliments and genuine kindness. Employees who are thanked regularly and appreciated for their contributions on the job:

- increase their individual productivity.
- increase engagement among their colleagues.
- are more likely to stay with their organization.
- receive higher loyalty and satisfaction scores from customers.
- have better safety records and fewer accidents on the job.[15]

It should be no surprise, then, that thanking and engagement reflects on the bottom line. Two Towers Perrin Consultancy's studies clearly illuminate the practical upshot of all this kindness. In a one-year analysis of 50 global companies, those businesses with highly engaged employees showed "19 percent increases in operating income and 28 percent growth in earnings per share. Contrast that with companies experiencing low employee engagement: they saw declines of 32 percent and 11 percent respectively in operating income and earnings per share.[16] In another study, this one conducted during the course of three years analyzing 40 multinational corporations, companies that scored high on employee engagement had operating margins that were more than 5 percent higher than companies with low employee engagement scores. Net profits were more than 3 percent higher too, causing a managing principal at Towers Perrin, Max Caldwell, to observe: "The organizations that have cracked the code understand that we're not just doing this to be nice; we're doing this for business reasons."[17]

The simplest, most direct, way to capitalize on the tremendous mutual benefits of appreciation is a take-off on the famous Nike slogan…

Just Say It

I can live for two months on a good compliment.

—Mark Twain

Thanking does not require an elaborate show of expensive gifts or time-consuming recognition programs in order to be effective. Instead, make others feel like winners by making liberal use of the simple compliment. Who doesn't feel energized and gratified when genuinely complimented? A simple "thank you" or "great job" is the verbal equivalent of a pat on the back. An old English proverb rightly observes that: "Kind words do not cost much. Yet they accomplish much." A kind word at the right time can turn a person's world around and give them the encouragement they need to persevere in the face of adversity. Salespeople will say that a simple compliment can boost them for days, and help them struggle through difficult sales months.

And a compliment is so easy to spread throughout your day as you go about your business. What kind words do you remember that have supported you along the way? What kind words can you plant today with someone else? Think about creating a positive work environment. Think of how you can unleash the verbal thank you on your employees and colleagues. Spotlight a different employee at each staff meeting. Make her the center of attention for a few minutes and have everyone on the team tell her what she has done well lately, and thank her for it. Lead off with the first thank you, and clap enthusiastically.

When you compliment others, particularly on something they have the ability to control or influence, you give them an immediate powerful boost and you help develop their self-esteem and confidence. When you acknowledge their efforts on the project they completed on time, you are affirming their value to the organization, not merely reflecting on this one incident of timeliness. A public compliment, praise, or positive observation can set a colleague's reputation and boost him toward his goals.

Beyond employer-employee relations, the effortless thank you can be doled out to spread these potent effects of kindness capital. Throughout the work day, there are many potential beneficiaries of a kind comment: the person delivering the bagels, the meeting facilitator, project colleagues, and prospective clients.

Politicians and other good speechmakers know the Power of Thanks. Virtually every good speech starts and ends with thanks, recognitions, and appreciation. In his 2008 State of the City Address, Mayor Loveridge credited much of the city's progress to the employees that work daily delivering city services. In a substantive, wide-ranging speech calling out action steps for the city and reflecting on past accomplishments, the mayor took the time to recognize one particular employee, a trash collector named Ray Perez, to thank him for his unerring loyalty and strong work ethic. A full-time driver since 1974, Ray had used only seven hours of sick leave in the previous 12 years. Obviously, when Ray was recognized at the event in front of his family, he felt good, and his motivation to continue to serve the residents of the city was enhanced. But more interestingly, the other 1,000 people in attendance also felt the warm glow of his acknowledgment. From the half-hour-long speech, the most commented-on and repeated portion was this small vignette about Ray and the thanks he received.

Not restricted to the professional realm, the everyday value of compliments is immense. The simple verbal compliment creates a glow of goodwill that reverberates well beyond the immediate recipient. The late Art Buchwald, columnist and political commentator, humorously illustrated the pervasiveness of these "side benefits" in a Washington Post column:

I was in New York the other day and rode with a friend in a taxi. When we got out, my friend said to the driver, "Thank you for the ride. You did a superb job of driving."

The taxi driver was stunned for a second. Then he said, "Are you a wise guy or something?"

"No, my dear man, and I'm not putting you on. I admire the way you keep your cool in heavy traffic."

"Yeh," the driver said and drove off.

"What was that all about?" I asked.

"I am trying to bring love back to New York," he said. "I believe it's the only thing that can save the city."

"How can one man save New York?"

"It's not one man. I believe I have made the taxi driver's day. Suppose he has twenty fares. He's going to be nice to those twenty fares because someone was nice to him. Those fares in turn will be kinder to their employees or shop-keepers or waiters or even their own families. Eventually the goodwill could spread to at least 1,000 people. Now that isn't bad, is it?"

"But you're depending on that taxi driver to pass your goodwill to others."

"I'm not depending on it," my friend said. "I'm aware that the system isn't foolproof, so I might deal with ten different people today. If, out of ten, I can make three happy, then eventually I can indirectly influence the attitudes of 3,000 more."

"It sounds good on paper," I admitted, "but I'm not sure it works in practice."

"Nothing is lost if it doesn't. It didn't take any of my time to tell that man that he was doing a good job. He neither received a larger tip nor a smaller tip. If it fell on deaf ears, so what? Tomorrow there will be another taxi driver whom I can try to make happy."

"You're some kind of a nut," I said.

"That shows how cynical you have become...."

We were walking past a structure in the process of being built and passed five workmen eating their lunches. My friend stopped. "That's a magnificent job you men have done. It must be difficult and dangerous work." The five men eyed my friend suspiciously. "When will it be finished?"

"June," a man grunted.

"Ah, that really is impressive. You must all be very proud."

We walked away. I said to him, "I haven't seen anyone like you since 'The Man of La Mancha.'"

"When those men digest my words, they will feel better for it. Somehow the city will benefit from their happiness."

"But you can't do this alone," I protested. "You're just one man."

"The most important thing is not to get discouraged. Making people in the city become kind again is not an easy job, but if I can enlist other people in my campaign...."

"You just winked at a very plain looking woman," I said.

"Yes, I know," he replied. "And if she's a school teacher, her class will be in for a fantastic day."

We certainly thrive on being appreciated. It is simply one of the kindest things you can do for another human being. But keep in mind that just as your simple compliments build others up, reckless utterances can tear down kindness capital.

Verbal Ammunition

Nobody ever gossips about other people's secret virtues.
                    —Bertrand Russell, Nobel Prize winning author

Never think that what you *do* is all that matters. Your utterances say more—and say more about you—than you may know. Everyday we have the choice to choose our words carefully, to send out positive and thoughtful missives that build kindness capital rather than break it down.

The old adage that downplays the power of negative words must be debunked. Remember the schoolyard claim "sticks and stones will break your bones, but words will never hurt you"? While it might have had some cachet in kindergarten, the notion that words don't directly affect us is a complete fallacy. Words can be more painful and have a more lasting negative impact than even the most well-placed physical blow. How many of us can still remember a cruel comment made many years ago?

Joseph Telushkin challenges us to avoid saying hurtful things for a 24-hour period in his book *Words That Hurt, Words That Heal.* This means not saying an unkind word *to* anyone (relatively easy) or *about* anyone (much more difficult). If you hold yourself strictly accountable for even the smallest unflattering comment, this is a very revealing exercise.

We are also challenged to assess how well we use the power of our words: "If someone were to pay you $0.10 for every kind word you ever spoke, and collect $0.05 for every unkind word, would you be rich or poor?" Adjusted for inflation, how would you be doing?

Then there is the other old adage, "If you can`t say something nice, don`t say anything at all." But how seriously do you take it? Many of us intuitively recognize that saying unkind things is wrong, but use joking as a shield to hide our negativity. If we are challenged or someone feels insulted by an unkind comment we've made, we often say, "I was just joking," or "Can't you take a joke?" Telushkin is especially critical of these "hidden" forms of unkind words and warns us away from the pervasiveness of gossip in particular. When talking about others, would you be willing to repeat what you'd said to the person's face? And, if not, what right do you have to say it at all? The result of snide comments, false jokes, and gossip is the same as that of direct verbal attacks—bad feelings, ill will, sullied reputations...and lost business.

An acquaintance who owns a retail shop recounted her run-in with the power of words. Tending the shop one afternoon, she helped serve a demanding client. The client required all available staff to bring her changes of clothing, shoes to try on with each outfit, and immediate responsiveness as she always did when she frequented the store. She made it worth their while when she left an hour later though by purchasing more than $1,500 of merchandise. When one of the sales clerks launched into a parody of the client, asking for just one more scarf to try on with her new outfit, the owner laughed out loud and threw in her own comment. It was a costly guffaw. A close friend of the client had coincidentally entered the store and overheard the mimicry. When she informed her friend later, the valuable client never returned.

Rumors and innuendo spread like wildfire—fast, and without care or concern for consequences. A statement, dropped casually with or without intent to harm, spreads at an exponential rate gathering fuel as it goes. Think of the "telephone game" that you played as a kid. Whoever was designated to start the game would make up a sentence and whisper it to the next child, who would pass it on to the next, and so on down the line until the last child would repeat it out loud for all to hear. Remember how hilariously distorted the sentence would be by the time it was passed on, edited both consciously and unconsciously, by many individuals? Now imagine a casually slanderous statement made that passes through the office cafeteria to suppliers, friends, and competitors.

A closing thought from Will Rogers: "Live so that you wouldn't be ashamed to sell the family parrot to the town gossip."

No Thanks

It's been my experience that the people who gain trust, loyalty, excitement, and energy fast are the ones who pass on the credit to the people who have really done the work. A leader doesn't need any credit... He's getting more credit than he deserves anyway.

—Robert Townsend, former CEO, Avis

Despite the disastrous ramifications of an unappreciative, negative work environment, and all the positive implications of a positive approach in business, there is nearly a complete dearth of thanking in the work world today. Some 65 percent of Americans surveyed in a 2007 Gallup Poll said that they had received no praise or recognition the previous year. That is, no one thanked them even once, said good job, or well done. Remarkable. Studies have confirmed that there are a lot more complaints than positive comments in most workplaces: eight negative to just one positive is the oft cited ratio prevalent in business today.

So why aren't thanking programs—formal and informal, large and small—*de rigeur* in every office place? And why don't individual professionals simply say thank you more often in all of their interactions? There is more than one reason.

First, thanking is sometimes avoided because it might seem to indicate agreement or satisfaction with the outcome or the process. Following difficult or contentious negotiations in my law practice, for instance, I was frequently tempted to just walk out of the room after winning concessions for my client, and making some compromises. I learned, however, that regardless of the outcome or process, shaking hands and saying "thank you" to the opposing attorney and his clients made everyone feel better, and preserved my reputation for future negotiations. If a customer service representative on the other end of the telephone was not able to resolve your issue to your satisfaction, but nonetheless treated you with respect, thanking them means "thanks for your time and effort," or "thank you for being a professional." (It can also mean thanks for being a live person rather than one of those horrible automated systems.) Thanking can simply acknowledge efforts and good conduct, rather than results.

Other times, people worry too much about getting credit. If employees' morale will flag and falter when they are unacknowledged, it is much worse when their ideas are expropriated. Sure the boss needs to be the front-runner on major projects and the figurehead for the organization, but beware of a tendency to claim credit where credit is not due. A study by Florida State University reported that 37 percent of respondents claimed that their supervisor failed to give credit when due.[18]

Instead, spread the true stories that credit your friends and rivals with their accomplishments. By speaking positively to, and about, others you also raise your own status. A word in defense of a colleague being criticized can preserve their reputation—and establish you as a strong leader. Giving thanks not only encourages the person you thank but also sheds an immediate and favorable light on you. Being willing to show kindness by thanking or complimenting a coworker for a job well-done shows that you subscribe to an abundance, rather than a scarcity, mentality. You are not afraid that another person looking good somehow takes away from your own success, and you have the confidence to spread the well-being of a public thank you. We'd do well to remember U.S. President Harry Truman's famous line: "You can accomplish anything in life provided you don't mind who gets the credit."

Next, efforts at more institutionalized thanking programs often fall into the "good intentions" barrier we looked at earlier. Many employers fret and fuss. They put in requests to their human resources departments and bring in numerous consultants to analyze and create programs, plans, and performance measures. These well-intended programs, caught up in budget cycles and cyclical downturns, rarely get implemented.

Finally, professionals are not always sure of whom to thank, or feel awkward about it. If whom to thank seems a bit of a puzzle, or you don't feel particularly thankful right now, try keeping a gratitude journal. A gratitude journal can be a separate document, or it can simply be daily notations in your daytimer or PDA. Keep track of things you are grateful for, from the small to the large. It might include being grateful that the crucial delivery of parts came in right on time. Or being pleased that your boss thanked you for the initiative you took to complete the report before it was due. Then, once a week go back to your notes and pick out a couple of the items and write a thank-you or recognition note to the person or organization that is associated with making you feel grateful.

Start thinking about how a gratitude journal will let you spread the warm glow of success throughout your office and among your clients and colleagues. You'll get the hang of it. In addition to helping you spread thanks in your professional environment, you'll find that keeping track of good things as they happen causes you to feel more positive and be more aware of the many good things in your life.

If you are failing to thank the people you work and do business with, you are missing out on the immense Power of Thanks.

Are the technological trappings of the modern day getting in your way?

Kindness Inhibitor:
The March of the Modern Day

Increasingly, we are all in our own virtual bubbles when we are out in public, whether we are texting, listening to iPods, reading, or just staring dangerously at other people.

—Lynne Truss, British author and humorist

The scope of e-commerce, cyber-infrastructure, and information technology is changing the way we do business. Business style looks very little like it used to. Increasingly, reliance on technology is itself a chief kindness inhibiting culprit, influencing business directions and outcomes.

The scale of everyday technology use is massive. Consider these statistics reported by Robert Emmons, author of *Thanks!*: "In 2005 it was estimated that 779 million cell phones would be sold, on which 1.7 billion people would be logging some 5.6 trillion minutes. By the year 2010 this number would more than double to 12.6 trillion minutes...[A]nd over 15 million personal digital assistants were expected to be shipped worldwide during that year [2005]."[19]

The very tools that make our work easier and faster also make it especially challenging to connect, personally and professionally. Reducing personal contact, in favor of so-called connecting with electronic gadgets that ostensibly help us communicate more efficiently, modern technology threatens kindness capital. Technology must become a relationship-*building* tool, rather than a distracting, isolating trap.

The Culprit: Cell Phones

You used to be able to pick up a phone and talk to people. That doesn't happen anymore. Now there's e-mail and automated switchboards.

—George Joseph, chairman of Mercury Insurance Company

The conductor was leading the Rhode Island Philharmonic orchestra through a powerful score during the opening performance when a cell phone started ringing. Several jangling rings later, the conductor stopped the music, turned to the audience, and spoke gruffly through gritted teeth into the microphone: "Answer your phone. Then turn it off." The audience applauded, the show went on, but the unthinking rudeness of the cell phone culprit left its mark.

The cell phone is perhaps the most ubiquitous and useful technology tool we have at our disposal. How did we ever get by without it? Yet, rivaled only by e-mail, it has tremendous potential for misuse and downright rudeness. In our rush to embrace the convenience of this tool, we have forgotten that some places are not meant for conversation. In dentist offices, in libraries, in schools, in hospitals, in the National Gallery of Art in Washington, D.C., and at the local performing arts center, "turn off your cell phone" signs are apparently needed to keep disrespectful cell usage in check. A study by researchers at Carnegie Mellon

University found that despite strict regulations, one-to-four cell calls were snuck in on each of 37 airplane flights studied.

The Atlantic Monthly coined the term "pandephonium" to describe the momentary confusion experienced when a cell phone rings unexpectedly in a group of people, and no one is sure just whose phone it is. Patting our pockets, opening our purses, and generally stopping all productive conversation until the ringing cell phone is found and answered, pandephonium accurately illustrates how far the cell phone has intruded into our daily lives. While allowing us to be in touch with anyone throughout the world at virtually any time or place, it has taken our attention and focus off of the people right in front of us and reduced the collective kindness capital in our workplaces and in our society at large.

More than half of Americans feel "impatient" or "unimportant" when a friend or coworker interrupts their conversation to take a cell call, according to a 2004 survey by Sprint. Dr. Ned Hallowell, author of *CrazyBusy*, coined the term "pizzle" (a combination of *puzzled* and just plain old *pissed off!*) for how he feels when someone he is talking to interrupts their conversation to take a cell call. When a professional makes a choice to take a cell call instead of continuing a live conversation or meeting, they unwittingly disrespect and diminish those present and can damage the deal.

Ironically, 97 percent of us characterize ourselves as either "very" or "somewhat" courteous on the cell phone. It is always the "other guy" on the cell phone disturbing your quiet lunch with an important business client, or surreptitiously taking a cell call in the middle of a conference session.

Simple guidelines can help. Keep your cell phone off in public. It is especially rude to use cell phones anyplace where other people are a captive audience, such as in a bus, restroom, restaurant, a grounded airplane, the grocery store line up, or a meeting. If you can do that, skip the rest of these guidelines and pat yourself on the back for using your cell phone respectfully. However, if there is truly an urgent reason (you will need to search your conscience as to what is really *urgent*) to have your phone on while in public, use discretion. Keep your phone on vibrate, let your companions know you are expecting a critical call, and apologize in advance for the anticipated interruption. Step away from others, if you cannot move to another room altogether, and keep your voice low. Always apologize to your companions when you return to the conversation or meeting to begin to rekindle the kindness capital you may have impacted, and do not expect them to recap what you missed.

A few years ago, my husband and I were on a remote spot on the Big Island of Hawaii walking hand-in-hand down a beautiful black sand beach, enjoying a light breeze, the clear sky, and the crashing ocean. Long before we saw him, we heard a young man on his cell phone walking toward us, complaining loudly and somewhat bitterly about his disappointment with the "lack of tranquility" of the island experience. We couldn't help but laugh at the irony.

When we cannot enjoy the beauty surrounding us, the company of our friends and colleagues, or the simple pleasure of a quiet moment, it is time to put down our cell phones and refocus on kindness capital.

The Culprit: E-mail

E-mail is ideal for distributing information to large groups of people. It's not the best way to have a conversation.

—Mike Song, author

One of the best descriptions of the pervasiveness of e-mail comes from Mayor Ron Loveridge, who has been heard exclaiming that "e-mail comes at you like confetti!" Like confetti, e-mail messages build up in massive clusters, are impossible to collect and organize, are time consuming to get rid of, and are generally bothersome when you get right down to it. Make sure the e-mail you write actually communicates effectively and represents you well within this blizzard. Even more importantly, knowing when to forgo electronic "communication" for real communication takes us on a brief examination of how to enable e-mail to build, rather than deplete, kindness capital.

When giving a speech to a group of educational office professionals, a younger member of the audience questioned my advice that an e-mail should be treated like a miniature letter. Just like a letter, I explained, an e-mail should have an opening salutation and ending statement, as well as a purposeful middle section, and should be concise, reflective, and communicate in a way of which you are proud. This young lady claimed that, like using the telephone, e-mail is more of an ongoing conversation and that, therefore, such structure is unnecessary. This illustrates the crux of a problem that inhibits e-mail from becoming a truly effective tool for anything other than the most superficial and routine of messages. Unlike telephone or face-to-face conversations, e-mail messages are devoid of verbal intonation and inflection, facial expression, and body language. Without visual and verbal cues to guide the recipient and augment the message, e-mails can seem abrupt and cold. And studies show that most of our intentions and meaning are gleaned from physical expression and vocal tone. How could typewritten communication, especially in the slapdash form that e-mail tends to be, possibly measure up?

People often use e-mail as an excuse for not actually communicating. Difficult topics and bad news can seem easier to deal with in an e-mail than in person and can mistakenly be confused with kindness. Misunderstandings frequently result from both an over-reliance on e-mail and a lack of care in composing messages. It is sheer folly to think that we can communicate effectively in the microsecond, willy-nilly kind of way we tend to throw e-mails together. We are notorious for sending disastrously poor e-mail, forgetting attachments, sending to the wrong recipients, and sending e-mails without proofreading, to name a few common foibles. The problem is exemplified by the story of a chief executive that appeared in the *Wall Street Journal*. He was composing an e-mail to four of his vice presidents about needing to fire the fifth, while at the same time trying to book a vacation in Mexico. To his great dismay he realized, just after pressing send, that he'd addressed the e-mail to all five of his vice presidents....

Some offices are fighting back to create greater civility and clearer communication, such as PBD Worldwide Fulfillment Services, in Alpharetta, Georgia. CEO Scott Dockter declared "no e-mail Fridays" and overall reduced e-mail use for his 275 employees. Four months into the experiment, despite some initial complaints and discomfort with face-to-face interpersonal communication, Dockter declared a success. The changes resulted in a 75 percent reduction in e-mail and increases in one-on-one discussions with correspondingly better teamwork. While not yet a full-scale phenomenon, reducing e-mail reliance and reemphasizing the value of the inter*personal* in communication is gradually catching on in other corporations and offices around the country.

Treat e-mail technology with care by following some simple tips. One sacred rule of e-mail is to keep your message brief—no more than three paragraphs. If you feel you need to write more, get up, walk over, and talk to your colleague in the next office. Make that telephone call to your client to convey what is too complicated to summarize easily in text or make an appointment to meet with your boss to discuss the next project. Avoid cc'ing more than a couple of people; again, know when to call a meeting or pick up the telephone instead. Before hitting "send," be sure that you would be comfortable to say this to a person's face and that you would be prepared for your words to circulate electronically around the entire office, to show up in the newspaper the next day, or worse, to appear in a legal proceeding.

Reply, if even briefly, to all e-mails you receive. If you've ever sent an e-mail inquiry to someone and simply had no response,

you know how unacknowledged and ignored—virtually absent—
you feel. A businessperson I know responds nearly instantaneously
to each e-mail with something as simple as "confirming" in the
text to simply let the sender know their e-mail is not lost in the
ether. But never, ever, participate in multiple "reply all" wars.

We are far too reliant on quick and easy forms of communication that unfortunately lack the "flavor" of real human interaction and fail to build kindness capital. To avoid the hit-and-run
effect of ill-used technology, take action to make your sure technology is working for you as a tool, not as a trap.

Practice Pointers

Men will stand a good deal when they are flattered.
—President Abraham Lincoln

You can readily turn the natural craving for appreciation into
an opportunity for mutual benefit. Build up others' self-esteem,
while reinforcing your positive influence and obtaining their best
efforts and highest performance using these kindness techniques:

- Choose at least one person each week to thank in
  recognition of something positive she does for you
  and your business, even if small.

- Send handwritten thank-you notes instead of thank-
  you e-mails whenever possible.

- Instead of a thank-you note, try a thank-you *book*.
  Buy a small inspirational book and write a note on
  the inside cover expressing your thanks. The recipient will think of you every time he looks at it.

- Thank especially those who might not get recognized regularly. Try, for example, a thank-you note to your long-time lawyer noting that you appreciate all she has done for you over the years; attorneys are some of the least acknowledged professionals.

- Compliment someone about a quality you think others may not notice about them.

- Give appropriate small gifts to business associates to thank them for good work.

- Tell your office assistant he or she did a great job, and be specific in your praise. Don't wait until Administrative Professionals Day to do it.

- Compliment someone in front of their supervisor or boss. Or send an e-mail to their boss remarking on something good the coworker did, and be sure to cc them.

- Compliment the boss. Often people at the top do not get positive feedback.

- Reevaluate your staff assignments. Is there a way to reassign duties so that you are playing to your staff's strong suits and making them feel like winners? Consider asking employees which projects they are interested in.

- Ensure your team has at least a 3-to-1 ratio of positive versus negative interactions on the job. Strive for 6-to-1 instead.

- Try the K.E.E.P.—kudos, empowerment, excitement, and promotion—formula that Robert Half International recommends for employee retention.

- Put anonymous kudos notes in colleagues' inboxes from time-to-time.

- Think about each valued employee and what might make them leave your office; see if you can proactively remedy it before it becomes a problem.

- At your next staff retreat, have each member of the staff anonymously write down three positive adjectives about each other staff member. Collect and collate the positive adjectives so that each person gets to take their list with them.

- Try no e-mail Fridays.

- Just do it!

Thanking touches the professional world in profound ways, bringing immediate and long-lasting benefits to both those who give and receive appreciation. Connecting is also an extremely compelling way to build kindness capital.

Chapter 6

The Power of Connecting

We elevate our own lives by helping others rise. The only way to push someone up a ladder is to climb with them, and so when you help others, your own life benefits.

—Les Brown, author

Mike Abrashoff knows there is no road to success that can be reached without connecting with others. When he became commander of his own ship in the U.S. Navy in 1997 at the age of 36, he employed a number of sound management techniques. But of all of the techniques he used, none was more important than connecting. Understanding that the golden rule principle is the basis for successful management, he told everyone on the ship: "It's *your* ship." He connected with them at a meaningful level, making each officer and enlistee feel a part of the mission. Each person was empowered with a sense of ownership and pride in *their* ship. Accordingly, under Mike's command, *their* ship became noted for its camaraderie, cost savings, record low turnover…and award winning performance.[1] Abrashoff knows that connecting creates buy-in and, accordingly, performance results.

Reid Hoffman, a Silicon Valley technology entrepreneur, credits the amassing of his sizable fortune to personal and professional contacts. Hoffman's relationships put him in the right place at the right time to invest early in some of the most successful technology start-up companies of our time, including PayPal and Facebook. These hard-to-come-by investment opportunities arose from his social (friends) and professional (colleagues and acquaintances) networks.

Hoffman's belief that his business track-record results more from the breadth of his network than his own particular business acumen led him to develop LinkedIn. LinkedIn, the successful online portal of some 22 million users is growing by 1.3 million users per month. Dedicated to helping busy professionals "virtually connect" with other professionals to expand their networks, share career options, and explore business opportunities, it puts into practice Hoffman's claim that connecting is the fast-track to accomplishment.

The essence of the Power of Connecting is found in Abrashoff and Hoffman's differing success stories.

Connecting with another person is a critically empowering and kind act. People want to contribute to something that matters and makes a difference even in a small way. Connecting becomes a business advantage when you create deep and meaningful professional relationships based on common ground and shared goals.

When you tap into the desire to contribute and help people see the value of their professional endeavors, you make them feel great *and* motivate loyalty and best efforts. This is what Abrashoff did.

Hoffman's lesson, on the other hand, lies in the expansiveness, rather than the depth, of connections. An extensive professional and personal network allows you to get to know and be known by others in a more peripheral way. Networking puts you in a position to do things for others, lots of others. You build irreplaceable kindness capital by connecting people to the resources and contacts they need to help them accomplish their professional goals. And your network works for you.

Create Common Ground

If there is any great secret of success in life, it lies in the ability to put yourself in the other person's place and to see things from his point of view—as well as your own.

—Henry Ford

As Mike Abrashoff knows, people are not a particularly rational lot. We are thinking, feeling, dynamically changing, and often confused, organisms.

Our right brains—responsible for our imagination and symbolism—are as, or more, important in business than our rational left brain analyses. In the words of Thomas Peters and Robert Waterman in their classic work, *In Search of Excellence*, on what makes companies excel: "We reason by stories *at least* as often as with good data. 'Does it feel right?' counts for more than 'Does it add up?' or 'Can I prove it?'"[2]

Treating your employees, coworkers, competitors, and suppliers as if they are primarily rational and analytical misses the opportunity to create deep connections with them.

Rather, find out what makes others tick. Figure out ways you can help them get what they want and need. Just what is the hidden ambition of the department secretary who also holds the key to getting on the boss's calendar? Don't assume it is simply her paycheck at the end of the week. What motivates your contract ad agency to produce the most innovative marketing for your company? Don't assume it is exclusively the payment at the end of the contract. Find ways to anticipate what inspires your boss; you'll have insights into how to help him achieve his true goals. When you connect with your colleagues and stakeholders, you do a tremendous service of kindness for them. It makes them *feel* good. They are happier, more satisfied, and fulfilled when they feel engaged and involved in a mission that meets their natural need for deeper meaning. Shared interests and common goals matter.

Create kindness capital by making everyone you associate with in your professional life part of "the plan." Go ahead and make the plan a grand one. Strive for big-picture, optimistic, high-impact goals for you, your business, and your people. Learn to leverage kindness to create meaningful connections with all of your stakeholders. Let your suppliers, contractors, and buyers understand your professional goals and the goals of the organization. Let others get swept up in your vision and shared goals.

Especially ensure that *all* of your employees feel part of the plan, not just peons or cogs in the machine. The formal organizational chart belies the connections and networks of relationships that exist in any organization. These largely social networks can make or break the effectiveness of a company. Management must find out what connects employees at all levels of their organization to ensure that the informal organizational structure supports the mission. Caring about employees is a hallmark of successful employee relations, believes Jeff Mooney, former CEO of A & W Restaurants who recommended that leaders "...love [y]our employees if you want them to love [y]our business."[3]

Sure, a positive employee culture includes the tangible perks provided and the appreciation received. But people also need to be part of something that matters and makes a difference, even if it's small. To motivate and obtain best efforts, employees need to know *why* they should strive for that sales goal or customer-service satisfaction rating. Rather than just telling them what to do, appeal to a goal and purpose, revealing how their efforts fit in to the bigger picture. Terrific loyalty and efforts are engendered to the professional or business that does this. Accordingly, customer service improves, productivity shoots up, and results are noticeable in the company ledgers.

Wondering how to create the common ground that touches off these feelings of well-being, and concomitant productivity?

Cultivate your empathy-ability.

Empathy, the ability to understand what others are feeling and see things from their perspective, is a critical factor in cultivating kindness capital. Take the focus off your own agenda and explore with interest and enthusiasm the uniqueness of your colleagues, employees, and all business stakeholders. Asking questions, listening to their answers, and developing your connectedness increases your ability to create real value for them.

When developing empathy, you learn to understand others: what makes them feel good and also what really matters to them. Learning others' motivations and fears enables you to be kind in very real and substantive ways. Daniel Goleman, in his foundational work on empathy, *Primal Leadership*, explains it like this: "…[E]mpathy is the sine qua non of all social effectiveness in working life. Empathetic people are superb at recognizing and meeting the needs of clients, customers, or subordinates."[4] With these insights, you can actively assist in advancing their goals and achieving their most closely held *dreams*.

Remember that everyone has an element of self-interest in operation much of the time. "What's in it for me?" one naturally wonders. You have to be able to answer that, be able to help others, and gain their best efforts. There are four central ways to develop empathy-ability and create the common ground that makes people feel good and perform even better.

1. Make a Marina

It is nice to be important but it is more important to be nice.

—Sir John Marks Tempelton,
businessman and philanthropist

Fortunately, you are not starting from zero in connecting with the people with whom you work. You already have a mutual interest in the profession, the particular issues and opportunities of the business, and a shared work environment. Marinas are an unexpectedly apt case study in developing empathy-ability in a shared work environment.

How, you might ask, can a marina be related to the office? Growing up with my dad's love of sailing, I spent some time around marinas as a kid. I knew, even then, that there was something special about the atmosphere at marinas. When my husband, John, and I bought a boat and a slip at a marina in Southern California, we rediscovered the unique nature of marina life. It teaches a key lesson in creating an empathetic environment, a lesson that extends well beyond the watery boundaries of these ocean havens.

Everyone in a marina has a built-in base of common ground, that is, their mutual interest in boating. But this alone does not account for the tightknit feelings of camaraderie, sociability, and helpfulness that dominate. Trading cheese over the side of the boat and borrowing supplies, the close quarters create and reinforce familiarity. The live-aboards look out for the weekend crew, and the weekenders bring baked goods from their homes to share with the yearlong residents. The unwritten rule of helpfulness is perhaps the most precious element of marinas. The best example of this is how nearby boaters come out to assist when a boat is coming in to its slip—to help tie off, avoid bang-ups, and then greet and welcome back to the dock, share information about the sail or cruise, and talk about weather conditions. Hierarchy and status is virtually nonexistent. We still don't know the career interests or job titles of most of our dock-mates. But we do know something about who they are as people, their aspirations and hopes.

The camaraderie and kindness found in marinas stems from the shared sense of a unique environment. Boaters in a marina know that their environment is extraordinary—their situation is a slice out of everyday life, most definitely not part of the "daily grind." In large part, chores are not done, routines are a foreign concept, schedules are not kept, and "island time" prevails. Marina-dwellers have a sense of a great adventure, a *shared* adventure.

Create this in your workplace by manufacturing an exciting environment with shared rituals, occasions, and bells-and-whistles. Some 21st-century office places have intentionally removed all walls and cubicles, creating a completely open-concept environment that encourages shouting out great ideas, trading office products, and sitting down cross-legged for an impromptu brainstorming session. Company teams are useful in creating a sense of adventure—sports, chess, bowling; whatever brings your staff together. Others have a roving Friday afternoon cocktail hour, some share charades to start their Monday morning staff meeting. Whatever it is that will fit in your business, make it something that creates a special environment...and allows people to get to know each other and create bonds.

2. Know Your People

The length and breadth of our influence on others are directly related to the depth of our concern for them.

—John Maxwell, best-selling
leadership author and speaker

Alongside the old axiom, "know thyself," should be the saying, "know thy people." Get to know your people—from those you work with directly to your business contacts and customers—by being approachable, someone with whom they can identify. Four winning leaders took somewhat different approaches to getting to know and empathize with their people.

Jim Collins's intensive research of 11 of the most successful Fortune 500 companies found that the leaders of these extraordinarily successful companies were ordinary people. These immensely powerful CEOs of multimillion-dollar companies were described by their employees with words such as gracious, mild-mannered, and kind.

"The good-to-great leaders never wanted to become larger-than-life heroes. They never aspired to be put on a pedestal or become unreachable icons. They were seemingly ordinary people quietly producing extraordinary results," said Collins.[5] Darwin Smith, CEO of the Kimberly-Clark paper-based consumer product company, was one of these leaders. By all accounts, an average guy with no self-important or big-wig executive attitude, he was someone employees could relate to. Darwin Smith...characterized by Collins as a man of extreme personal humility, leveraged that down-to-earth approach well, garnering cumulative stock returns during his 20-year tenure from 1971 to 1991 that were 4.1 times the general market.

Julie Stewart, president and CEO of IHOP Corporation, recalled her wisest move as being one of spending time with her line-employees. She spent much of 2006, her first year as CEO, in the kitchens and on the floor of countless IHOP restaurants across the United States. Stewart got to know the franchisees and employees so they saw her as a flesh-and-blood person, rather than an icon at the top of the hierarchy. Getting to know the people behind the brand has made a big difference in IHOP's recent revitalization efforts, evidenced by total revenues that increased significantly from $350 million in 2006 to $485 million in 2007.

UPS leadership also knows how to connect with employees. The UPS philosophy of promoting internally is well known, and has served them well. Most of the founders, owners, and upper management started in operations, many as deliverymen. Working shoulder-to-shoulder, bonds were established and the vision of the company grounded in all levels of the organization. As the organization grew, management established a newsletter called "Big Idea" that looked for and included ideas and tips from *all* levels of the company and served as another reminder to the employees that the company represented a shared opportunity. With a market capitalization of $42.6 billion, its extensive list of national recognitions includes awards for social responsibility, corporate citizenship, customer service and loyalty,…and employee satisfaction.

Patrick O'Brien, president of Johnson Outdoors, a recreation clothing and products company with gross profits of nearly $175 million annually, captured the mutual value of getting to know the people you work with when he said that "Getting to know people individually is more important now than ever. If you have that one-hour personal conversation at the start with someone, six months later, on a Friday at 4 p.m., they're jumping with you."[6] Taking the time to talk with employees in an unstructured environment—outside of performance evaluations, staff meetings, and project planning meeting—is crucial to understanding them and in developing connectedness and buy-in.

These four leaders demonstrate that when you connect with your people personally, they will thrive professionally—investing their best efforts, time, and talents in your business.

Nevertheless, managers and business owners often shy away from real contact and getting to know the people with whom they work. Adhering to a "professional distance," they fail to learn their peoples' personal likes and dislikes, avoid joking and laughing together, and generally keep the entrenched hierarchy in place. More than half of employees surveyed in the United States and globally gave their senior leaders low marks on empathy and reported that their senior management treats them "as if we don't matter."[7] Keeping the guard up professionally makes it hard for employees to bond with the boss, and harder still for them to see the purpose, beyond their paycheck, of the companies' activities.

One corporate executive from a major cruise line characterizes the corporate facade as "checking your personality at the door." While cruise liners sound swanky and glamorous, their corporate life can be as neutral and dulled-down as any stodgy accounting firm of your imagination. E-mails at this cruise line corporation's head office seem virtually anonymous because they are so formulaic, with no hint of personality or emotion. With no warmth or affection displayed, this executive said, one e-mailed set of instructions is much the same as the next, and could literally be coming from anyone. The "corporate man" syndrome makes it exceedingly hard to establish connections. When people do not know who they are working for and working with, they have less loyalty, less motivation to excel.

With an empathy approach, you will often find that there is more common ground between you and others than you initially realized. But cultivating empathy will not be effective without a genuine interest in others. Empathy must be real and is never obsequious or fawning. People *will* notice if your words are saccharine-sweet but fail to match your actions. Any pretense of put-on caring tends to fall flat. Jimmy Johnson, former coach of the Dallas Cowboys and the Miami Dolphins says, "The only thing worse than a coach or CEO who doesn't care about his people is one who pretends to care. People can spot a phony every time. They know he doesn't care about them, and worse, his act insults their intelligence."[8]

A hallmark of genuine empathy involves learning the skill of actively attending to others.

ACTIVE ATTENDING. Paying attention, attending to others, makes others feel great—it taps into that deep-seated need to be recognized that we looked at in Chapter 5. Ask questions and really listen to the answers. Really listening to understand others' interests and concerns allows you to respond effectively. It may be a small part, a nugget, of a larger conversation that gives you information and ideas that can help you create a connection.

All too often we ask a "pro forma" question and then tune out the answer, not being truly interested in the response. President Franklin Roosevelt reportedly pulled the leg of guests in a receiving line when, one evening, he presumably tired of shaking hands and vapid chit-chat. He tested guests' listening skills by throwing out a shocking statement said in a jovial voice tone exclaiming, "I murdered my grandmother this morning." As the urban legend goes, while most were on autopilot replying "Oh yes, how nice!" and the like, one aware woman was said to have caught his attention when she replied mildly: "I'm sure she had it coming to her."

Pay attention to all people from all walks of life, not just the big clients, the main suppliers, the majority shareholders. Assume value in others' ideas. There is good reason to do so: Peters and Waterman's groundbreaking study of America's most successful corporations found that these companies listened and learned from their customers and employees alike. "Many of the innovative companies got their best product ideas from customers. That comes from listening, intently and regularly."[9] It is not just the highly paid consultants and industry experts who deserve our attention…and who can lead you to the next big breakthrough in customer service or innovation.

Mike Abrashoff practiced what he called "aggressive listening," starting with his ship's youngest sailors. Typically given the grunt work of chipping and painting, the sailors felt frustrated that they were wasting their time. When Mike took the time to listen with empathy, he learned that simply replacing the rusting hardware with stainless-steel equipment eliminated that costly and time-consuming chore—and boosted the morale of the sailors. Daniel Goleman's analysis showed how listening makes for an empathetic leader: "They seem approachable, wanting to hear what people have to say. They listen carefully, picking up on what people are truly concerned about, and they respond on the mark. Accordingly, empathy is key to retaining talent."[10] Empathetic individuals and companies know that actively attending to their people makes them talent magnets—drawing in customers and employees alike.

The best leaders are approachable. They know that their employees and customers need to be able to identify with them, so they create a genuine sort of intimacy with whomever they speak. Another way to create a strong sense of connectedness and commitment to the goals of the organization is even more direct.

3. Buy In

There are only two options regarding commitment. You're either in or out. There's no such thing as a life in-between.

—Pat Riley, basketball coach and player

Sometimes the simplest way to create buy-in is to allow your people to actually *buy in*. Plenty of companies, from small to large, offer stock options to create that "skin in the game" feel—Starbucks and UPS are two such organizations.

Howard Schultz, CEO of Starbucks, has consistently cultivated and kept the best baristas and managers in the retail industry. In addition to creating a positive work environment, it offers employees the opportunity to purchase stock options. Knowing the value of bought-in employees, from senior executives to full-time line staff: "Starbucks executives continue to respectfully and willingly share profits with their people. Through this sharing, partners appreciate the direct link between their effort and the success of the business enterprise."[11]

UPS offered equity to more than one-tenth of its employees in 1927, including drivers, deliverymen, and the rank and file. Knowing that company success is not solely reliant on brilliance in the executive office, UPS has consistently connected with its middle management and non-management staff. When the company's shareholder base was 602 people in 1936, 247 of those company owners were drivers, helpers, mechanics, washers, and porters. Today, all employees are still encouraged to invest in the company by buying its now publicly traded stock. A sense of skin in the game, plus a promote-from-within policy, makes the feeling of ownership at UPS high. And it shows. UPS reports a very low turnover rate, a mere 8 percent, among full-time managers worldwide.[12]

Whether you can offer stock options or not, there are plenty of ways to create this sort of buy-in: performance-based bonuses, incentives, and shared special-event celebrations when certain markers are achieved.

The result? Employees are invested, literally and figuratively, in their work and more importantly in *shared* outcomes.

4. Yearning for "Yes"

If you can learn to say "yes" to every client, boss, and new business prospect, you'll be able to skip climbing up the corporate ladder and take the express elevator instead.

—Linda Kaplan Thaler and Robin Koval,
advertising executives and authors

The most common approach to business success is to be tough, make liberal use of the word no, and focus on solitary achievement of goals. Many counsel the wisdom of turning things down in your personal and professional life. Sure, with this approach you'll avoid overextending yourself or being taken advantage of, but you will also miss tremendous opportunities to connect and build your kindness capital.

One of the simplest, yet most revolutionary, ways to be kind and empathetic is by agreement. When you can say "yes" to at least *some aspect* of what others want, you expand the possibilities for partnership and create probabilities for success.

Yes is truly the most powerful word in the English language. Using it affirms, reassures, and establishes you as someone who can be trusted to care about others' best interests. In business dealings, always try to lead with a yes, even if you cannot end with one. When negotiating a deal, find something you can agree to, even if a small transactional point, and start there. It might sound like: "Yes, we would like to buy 500 computer chips at the price you stated." Then, with all parties warmed up and goodwill established, you can enter into the part where you need to get concessions or different deal terms. By starting with a yes, trust is established and the door opened for *mutually* beneficial negotiations.

Better yet, in negotiations try to ascertain what they really want *most*. Use your empathy-ability, including probing for information and actively listening to the answers, to find out what really makes your business partner tick. Then see if you can give it to them as negotiations expert Ronald Shapiro counsels: "Often, the best way to get what you want is to help the other side get what they want."[13] Not incidentally, you must also know what *you* really want. That might take some introspection and thoughtfulness as to what the picture of success looks like for you in the specific instance. When you get most of what you want and need, and they get at least their prime goal met, you both walk away satisfied with kindness capital increased all around.

Here's how "yessing" your way to success might look on an average Friday afternoon. Your boss approaches you to stay late on a Friday evening to do damage control on a project that isn't even your responsibility. Consider the motivating factor. Is the boss simply being unreasonable and inconsiderate about your private time? Unlikely. Go deeper, ask questions, and listen to the answers to connect and empathize with her. You'll likely find that the boss had gotten sidetracked and the project is now dangerously lagging behind schedule—and a crucial presentation to venture capitalists has been moved up to Monday afternoon. Find a way to say "yes," that you would be happy to help her with the deadline. Then set your own terms. Let her know that you'll bring your computer with you on your weekend in the mountains and get that chart done for her by Monday morning. It may mean that you are designing a spreadsheet while sipping a glass of wine from your patio overlooking the sunset on Sunday evening. Your "yes" means that both you and your boss's primary needs are met.

The Tamale Factory, a Mexican food joint in Riverside, California, knows the value of "yessing" their customers. The cafeteria-style restaurant was packed with lunch customers when my business associate and I arrived at the cash register with our trays laden with food. When I saw a sign saying "cash or check only," I had a sinking feeling as I made a mental inventory of my wallet and realized I had neither. With lunch totaling just under $18, I faced a quandary. I certainly did not want to have my business associate feel obligated to pay, and I most certainly did not want to have to try to return our food.

The cashier, one of the owners in this small family-owned restaurant, recognized my sinking expression and uncertain fumbling in my wallet and quickly offered "Just come back later, in a day or two, and you can pay for it then." Without other alternatives at hand, I gratefully accepted, sat down with my companion and had a fruitful meeting over a delicious lunch.

What the Tamale Factory proprietor Josie Hornback risked by finding a way to tell me yes was a mere $18 lunch if I had not come back. Josie's daughter and business partner, Naomi Avila, told me that some other businesspeople don't think they are very good businesspeople because of such practices. But what they gambled and gained was a loyal customer. By saying they could help me, making me feel at home, and saving me from embarrassment, they connected with me in a lasting way. What they couldn't have known was that I was to become a regular downtown diner, that I regularly take people out to lunch with me, and that I occasionally have the opportunity to suggest restaurants to cater large events. For the Tamale Factory, it is a genuine caring that motivates them but, "If you love your customers and take care of them, they come back...and bring their friends," acknowledged Naomi. Going out on a limb and taking that risk created a business benefit for them. (I later learned that they rather frequently offered this honor system option and that they *always* get paid back.)

Undoubtedly, you have at least a few instances where you have been "yessed." Remember how good it felt? Think of ways you can create this attitude in your professional life; see the practice tips at the end of this chapter for ideas. Establishing this special connection with a customer or client solidifies their loyalty and often creates a grassroots public relations network.

When you develop your empathy-ability, you not only know how to be kind to others in the ways that deeply matter to them, but you also learn how to turn the Power of Connecting to your advantage. Focusing next more on breadth, creating vibrant networks also advances the Power of Connecting.

Nuanced Networking

...Labor markets are thoroughly permeated by networks so that most of us are as likely to get our jobs through whom we know as through what we know.

—Robert Putnam, political scientist and author

Networks, the webs of contacts we create, have *immense* value. Professional networks deserve our attention well beyond the ubiquitous Chamber of Commerce events and much more often than during February's International Networking Week. The essence of effective networking is uncovering avenues for mutual benefit that increases kindness capital.

Expanding your personal and professional network creates opportunities for cooperation, and puts you in the position to be of assistance to others. Getting to know others creates ties and shared bonds, and develops mutual likeability.

Nuanced networking, then, focuses on getting to know others and finding ways to aid them. What are their hopes and dreams, and how can you, even in some small way, help them get there by being a "connector"?

I suspect that Paul Capetelli, peace officers standards and training executive director in Sacramento, California, is a "connector." Connectors, named so by Malcolm Gladwell in his best-selling book *The Tipping Point*, are special people with vast and well-developed networks. These networking geniuses function as a sort of professional lubricant, connecting us to each other across vastly different socioeconomic realms and geographically distinct locations. The best connectors are simply naturals, they don't think of it in terms of a business strategy. They just do it because they enjoy other people and like to help out.

Capetelli shared one of his networking techniques with me after I presented an image management seminar to a group of law enforcement personnel. At events and meetings, he keeps his Blackberry close at hand. If someone mentions needing a particular type of service or contact with a professional provider, Paul unobtrusively pulls out his Blackberry, rolls through his extensive list of contacts and resources, and e-mails the contact information to the person on the spot. Sometimes he acts in an intermediary role by sending an introductory e-mail to smooth the way.

Networking also positions you to be that next business partner. Meeting and getting to know people makes it more likely that they will be comfortable to do business with you, when and if that time should come. So much of the 21st century's global commerce is conducted through networks that one cannot expect to succeed in business without some skill at networking. "Indeed, it has been shown that our lifetime income is powerfully affected by the quality of our networks," says acclaimed political scientist and author Robert Putnam.[14] We prefer to do business with people with whom we are familiar and share values; people we know. Once you have established a comfort level and the foundations of trust, you can do business more quickly. You can skip the red tape, avoid the battery of legal and accounting experts, and short-circuit some of the costly preliminary due diligence in business deals, if you already know and trust each other.

With all the benefits at stake, you will not want to force the process. Avoid stigmatizing networking by lapsing into "glad-handing" or "speed networking." Indiscriminately or aggressively handing out business cards is the kind of behavior that has given networking an undeserved bad name. As corporate etiquette expert Jacqueline Whitmore says, "Be a farmer, not a hunter." Rather, think of networking as simply getting to know people, learning about what matters to them, and what makes them tick. To practice the nuanced type of networking, experiment with avoiding the exchange of titles and credentials. Instead, try connecting with your new acquaintance about interests and hobbies.

Make friends first; think business later.

Fortunately, even those less naturally adept at connection-making can become a connector, or at least learn to engage in strategic networking. The best networkers know that an acquaintanceship, let alone a deeper professional relationship, does not happen instantaneously.

Little Things That Count

You can make more friends in two months by becoming interested in other people than you can in two years by trying to get other people interested in you.

—Dale Carnegie, businessman, author, and philanthropist

Fortunately, the little things do count when establishing a business relationship. Take note of others' interests. Emphasize those things that you share in common. Reinforcing your similarities will create a connected, strong network with goodwill that lasts.

Mutually productive networking that effectively creates kindness capital follows five principles.

1. Prepare

Before anything else, preparation is the key to success.
—Alexander Graham Bell

When you want to add someone to your network, you'll need to do your homework. Identify who you want to get to know, and then find out all you can about him or her (within the boundaries of respecting his or her personal information, of course). Usually a simple Internet search provides more than enough information.

What data is publicly available on this person's company or product? How is the company doing? Is it highly dependent on market fluctuations, such as real estate? This will give you insight into the kinds of issues he or she is currently facing.

Scan the Internet also for information on his career type. If you learn that he or she is an architect, don't stop with that one piece of information. Rather, find out what it means to be an architect—how much schooling likely attended, and what kind of mindset he or she might be coming from.

Your network-building efforts should include the personal too; typically, the 21st-century business environment makes little distinction between the personal and professional realms.

We transition from boardroom to golf course to pub to dinner, often seamlessly, and with boundaries frequently blurred. What are their hobbies? To what teams and associations do they belong? This type of information, too, gives you insights that you can use to assist and establish a connection with them.

Fortunately the social media that characterizes the 21st-century makes doing your homework exceptionally easy. Chances are the Web presence of a professional or company extends beyond a Website and includes a blog; a profile on Facebook, LinkedIn, or MySpace; or a Twitter presence. These forums offer tremendous insights into your new acquaintance.

The information you glean forms the basis for an element that is absolutely crucial in nuanced networking: figuring out how to create value for your contact.

2. Create Value

Relationships are all there is. Everything in the universe only exists because it is in relationship to everything else. Nothing exists in isolation. We have to stop pretending we are individuals that can go it alone.

—Margaret Wheatley, PhD,
writer and management consultant

Cofounder and chief executive of PayPal, Peter Thiel knows efficient, effective networking: "I pay a lot of attention to building relationships. Part of how to create a lot of value and goodwill in the system is by doing something that is a little bit of work for me and massively valuable for you."[15]

Networking affords terrific opportunities for developing kindness capital. One of the simplest ways is to connect others to the people who can help them. With the mere sending of an e-mail, picking up of the telephone, or gathering for a cup of coffee, you can create immense value for other people by connecting them with the people and resources they need and want. Networking actually creates more value, more goodwill in the system, than was there before. Giving, and receiving, is part of the cycle of professional networks.

Take Thiel's advice and it doesn't have to be labor intensive, either. Here's how it works. An acquaintance of mine, Andrea de Leon, a PR consultant to DHL, was facing irate residents in the city of Riverside, California, angry over the new DHL hub disturbing their sleep with nighttime flights. Andrea was also facing demands from her client DHL, which was looking for solutions to calm the public outrage that was threatening its hub's very livelihood. Staging a dinner to try to find the positive in a contentious situation, Andrea invited me to represent the city and my husband, John, to represent the community college district in which he is a dean, and look for a way to emphasize the positive in DHL's presence by offering training programs and upwardly mobile careers for local students. Over dinner with the executive vice president of DHL and other top brass from the region, I took the opportunity to do what I could to solidify Andrea's role with DHL. In addition to being noticeably warm to her, I worked into the conversation the depth and breadth of her community knowledge and expertise and emphasized how important that would be in healing the current rift. While not skirting the issue of the upset caused by the noisy night-flights, I simultaneously complimented and strengthened Andrea's role. With very little effort on my part, I created great value for her…and a lifelong ally for me. It is as simple as that.

Don't worry about keeping score in your networking relationships. Rather, focus on networking that creates value. Rest assured that each time you create kindness capital, there is more kindness capital for you to draw upon.

3. Create "Weak Ties"

…[W]e live in a world in which no one is more than a few handshakes from anyone else. That is, we live in a small world. Our world is small because society is a very dense web.

—Albert-Laszlo Barabasi, author

It is tempting to languish in our conversational comfort zones. For most of us, it is easier and less stressful to converse with people with whom we are already familiar. Walking in to a business reception, we naturally greet and gravitate toward people we know. You must break free from this alluring comfort zone both so that you can be of assistance to more people and so that you can avail yourself of the information and resources that social contacts bring to bear.

Diversify, get to know people who don't look, act, or think like you. Go up and down the corporate ladder, getting to know everyone you can. Remember that we are all simply people— don't let fancy titles and status stop you from networking with "higher ups." And, similarly, don't miss out on connecting with those lower on the totem pole. People are fascinating, and you never know where they will end up. Bring people together. Go out and meet people.

Failure to break your comfort barriers results in an abbreviated network. And you don't want to miss out on the advantages a lot of acquaintances bring, especially if you are looking to upgrade your job.

In fact, a seminal study by sociologist Mark Granovetter found that it is our acquaintanceships that matter more than our friendships in connecting us to professional opportunities. Our informal acquaintances—weak social ties—provide an effective bridging mechanism to other social and professional networks that we would likely not have access to through our close friends, who tend to run in the same circles and know the same folks we already know. Traditional applications and job search methods have their place when looking to make a professional move but have nowhere near the value of connections: "...personal contacts are of paramount importance in connecting people with jobs."[16]

The result? Better jobs, faster.

Managers looking for jobs who tapped into the information provided by their weak ties found better, higher income, higher prestige positions, and they found them more quickly.

Networking provides terrific opportunities to benefit from others' contacts, but you have to get over your barrier to accepting help. Many professionals fail to realize the latent benefit of their networks because they simply don't ask. They don't ask for help when they truly need it. They don't ask for favors or referrals and instead wait, hoping for help to be offered. Aside from your closest family and friends, you cannot sit back and merely hope that someone notices your assets or your predicament. You must be willing to be bold to take advantage of the value of networking.

Trust in the power of networking and don't assume that anything is beyond your reach if you ask. The six degrees of separation experiment, conceived by Stanley Milgram, a Harvard professor during the 1960s and psychologist, illustrates the phenomenon, using a chain letter. Milgram posed the research question of how many connections it would take random individuals living in Omaha, Nebraska, to get a package into the hands of the targets, an unknown stockbroker working in Boston or a woman living in Sharon, Massachusetts. Assuming the participant didn't know the target on a first name basis they were instructed to get the package to a person they did know on a first-name basis, and thought would have a better chance of being connected to the target. And so, passed on through the mail and hand-to-hand, the experiment came up with the surprising result that, on average, it took only five or six people to get the package to the anointed target. Six degrees of separation has been cited since this fascinating research was turned into a play and then a popular movie by the same name, bringing this rather intricate sociological study into the mainstream (and incidentally resulting in wrongly interpreting Milgram's results by moving from interconnectedness in the United States to a supposed six degrees of separation from anyone in the entire world).

Milgram's six degrees research has been further analyzed by Malcolm Gladwell in the *Tipping Point*, providing an additional conclusion that proves the strength of weak ties. Half of the letters delivered to the targets came through the same three people. More than a hundred randomly selected people living in a randomly selected Midwestern city sent out letters that filtered to their destination point by the same three people. Thus the value of *certain connections*, or more specifically certain *connectors*, is important. Capitelli is one such connector. I bet you know a few too. If you have a question about a service provider, need some information about an organization, wonder what is happening with so-and-so, this is the person you automatically call. This person, the connector, seems to know everyone, or at least knows someone who does. You know, they actually might!

4. Make the Most of a Meal

> *In building a network, remember: Above all, never, ever disappear.*
> —Keith Ferrazzi, marketing and sales consultant, author

Mealtime is a prime opportunity for networking, building, and reinforcing these all-important social acquaintances, your weak ties. However, most of us are fast-food junkies. While we may not actually pick up from our local McDonalds, we engage in fast-food dining nearly each and every mealtime. We eat standing up, we eat in the car, we eat while checking our Blackberries, or hunched over our e-mail, dropping sandwich crumbs into our keyboards. Fast-food flies in the face of what our forbearers taught us of both dining etiquette and good business. A solitary, fast-paced meal is a squandered opportunity. And we'd be wise to take another look at how mealtimes can work for us to develop the network that provides business opportunities galore.

Dining etiquette is often mistaken for a morass of confusing and pedantic rules. Which fork, which glasses, which way to pass, where to put the pesky napkin, and other pretentious rules seem to taunt the uninitiated and lie in wait to trip us up. But dining etiquette really harkens back to a whole different era in which dining was intended as an event, a tradition. Mealtime provided a reliable way to connect with others. The dining room was the site of both family meals and dinner parties with stimulating and leisurely discussions. A good meal was the setting for conversation and connection, and provided a venue for more than food. But, through time, dining habits of this continent have coarsened, becoming a way to get fed rather than to feed the soul. Calories are consumed, calories are counted, dishes are set and cleaned, but the dialogue that used to typify a meal is not counted among the mealtime goals.

The seemingly fussy rule of putting your fork and knife down between bites—that is between each and every bite—is really a way of slowing down the dining process to allow you to connect with others. When you actually follow this rule, you see how quickly your attention moves from the food to the person with whom you are dining. When taking a bite is punctuated by a pause where you can make eye contact and converse, you start to see the whole purpose of mealtime morph from caloric intake to quality time. Indeed, the proper place setting itself is actually carefully orchestrated and designed to optimize eye contact with your dining partner and to minimize confusion and accidents.

Glasses to the right, bread and butter to your left keeps the way clear to see your companion. Becoming familiar with the place setting is a good way to focus on the conversation at hand, rather than fumbling with the fork and knife.

And with some 40 percent of business still being conducted at a meal, how you comport yourself at the dining table, and how you combine personal and professional conversation are of major significance. Studies show that executive recruiters pay close attention to food *faux pas*, judging many an otherwise excellent candidate unfit by their clumsy dining habits. And more than your etiquette savvy is shining through at business meals. In *Unwritten Rules of Management*, Raytheon CEO Bill Swanson explained his observations of people through his "Waiter Rule": "A person who is nice to you but rude to the waiter, or to others, is not a nice person." How you handle the entire dining experience, from checking your coat to taking the check, reflects not just your familiarity with business practices but your level of kindness capital.

Building a relationship is still the primary focus of any successful business interaction, especially at a mealtime. Meals are not for closing deals. When sharing a meal with a potential business associate, keep in mind that, until recently, the rule of thumb was to wait until the after-dinner coffee was served before bringing up business. Even now, business should generally be a side dish, not the entrée, of the mealtime talk.

Making the meal take a backseat to the meal*time* itself is the epitome of considerate, and constructive, dining.

5. Fine Follow-Up

The day on which one starts is not the time to commence one's _preparation_.

—Anonymous

What you do *after* you meet someone is as important as your first impression. To cement a relationship, to move it from a fleeting introduction to an acquaintanceship you can rely on, your follow-up is critical.

After meeting someone, take a moment to jot down his or her interests. On the back of their business card, in your address book or wherever makes sense for you, these notes will form the basis for follow-up.

It is easier than ever in the 21st century. Younger professionals, especially, utilize the social media to connect. Drop your new contact a note on their LinkedIn profile, send an e-mail or text message, or pop on to his or her blog and get into the conversation.

But don't disregard the highly effective and efficient, old-fashioned written correspondence. *What?!* Handwritten notes, you exclaim? Increasingly overlooked, notes may initially seem outdated, slower, and even redundant to e-mail and the social media methods. But as opposed to e-mails, notes are not glanced at and deleted in a mere 15 seconds. Written notes make us slow down, and they tell us that this is important, this *matters*.

Write thank-you notes. Thanking gets you noticed, tapping into the extraordinary Power of Thanks. Smart professionals send thank-you notes to their networks as often as possible: I know of one person who writes five thank-you notes each day. Savvy professionals on their way up write thank-you notes in the interview process. Research done by Accountemps indicates that 88 percent of executives believe a thank-you note to an interviewer can influence a hiring decision.[17]

Tear out an article on a topic of mutual interest from the newspaper or a magazine and send it with a short note to someone you met at an event. Referencing a discovered mutual interest in snorkeling in a note to a new acquaintance, you are reminding them of both your thoughtfulness and of your shared interest.

Inherent in good follow-up is follow-*through*. Give your new contact access to you. Be available to let the person to get to know you: go out for lunch, invite them to your office, grab a cup of coffee. If you say you are going to do something, you *must* do it. Nothing will turn your new contact off more than an unfulfilled promise. Providing a reference, making an introduction, or making the call you promised functions as glue that ultimately cements a relationship. Remember to focus on creating value for your new contact.

Above all else, make time to network. Your professional success depends on it.

Through building your empathy-ability and conducting strategic networking, you connect with people at important levels, build kindness capital, and make them feel good. Plus, you gain valuable insight and form relationships that make doing business a natural next step.

Why, then, doesn't everyone connect with others in a mutually beneficial, increasingly networked business model that sends everyone's goodwill, kindness capital, and profit margins soaring? The answer lies at least partially in the competition conundrum.

Kindness Inhibitor:
The Competition Conundrum

Life is much less a competitive struggle for survival than a triumph of cooperation and creativity.

—Dr. Fritjof Capra, physicist and author

The urge to compete seems to be virtually hardwired into our very beings. Like all creatures on this planet, we appear instinctively conditioned to fight to survive and to thrive. The competition to thrive is particularly insidious in North American society where the sense of "besting" others in the pursuit of success has become a badge of honor. The 24/7 multinational marketplace can be a pressure-cooker. With the global economy raising the opportunities for worldwide profits and in a climate where "more, better, and faster" is the mantra, it is easy to slip into competition overdrive.

Particularly in the early stages of a career, it is easy to succumb to the "climbing the corporate ladder" mentality. Often fresh out of college and eager to pay off debts or accumulate wealth to prove adulthood and independence, young professionals storm into their new careers with a vengeance. Needing to prove that years of schooling, student loans, hard work, and dreaming of the "real world" were not in vain, young professionals sometimes go in strong—too strong. First years of a career are often all about posturing and positioning for future promotions.

Even in later career stages, the drive to compete is a strong force. "For most people, life is not that competitive, and yet we seek out competition anyway," says professor of psychology Charles P. Ewing at the State University of New York at Buffalo.[18]

Added to this competitive compulsion is the lingering fear that showing kindness will reduce, or even eliminate, our chances of thriving. This kindness inhibitor runs deep and has its basis in the nice guys finish last myth. The perception that competition is a more successful strategy in business is remarkably prevalent, even in light of the studies that have proven otherwise. A *Business Week* poll of 2,500 American managers and executives reported that an extremely talented, yet uncompetitive, person was expected by only one-third of respondents to be more likely to get ahead. The modestly talented, but highly competitive, person was the favored winner by two-thirds.[19]

However, make no mistake: Cooperation is not a poor business strategy. Rather, the best and most effective way to make our own mark is to cooperate, not compete, with others. We've already seen how being likeable, garnering reciprocal favors, and building networks creates tremendous mutual professional opportunities.

So skip the competitiveness, and let's figure out how to work *with* the competition.

Cooperate With the Competition

Am I not destroying my enemies when I make friends of them?
—Abraham Lincoln

Niceness is as disarming a strategy in business as there is. Complimenting and connecting with your competition, even your adversaries, is a terrific way to conduct business.

I could say that you should help your competitors out of the goodness of your heart. It certainly reflects their intrinsic value and your abundance mindset. But we are on the lookout for *mutual* benefits—ways to capitalize on kindness in business. Fortunately, there are at least three ways that assisting and collaborating with your competition benefits you, too.

First, sometimes called "co-opetition," the business world is getting wise to a healthy blend of competition and cooperation—competing on some initiatives while cooperating and working as partners wherever practically possible and mutually advantageous. SAP and Microsoft successfully tried out co-opetition when they collaborated on their "Duet" line of products, and yet remain rivals for overall market share. This groundbreaking collaboration was launched in 2005, the first between these two major companies, and enables users to access SAP business processes via Microsoft Office. Shai Agassi, a member of SAP's executive board, offers a customer-driven explanation: "The customer base wants us to stay gentleman, so that's what we do. We keep the competition inside a fence and don't let the blood leak out."[20] Similarly, Red Hat, a Linux software company, considers IBM a co-opetition partner, even while it sells competing software.

Trevor Pickett, owner of luxury leather goods brand Pickett based in England, also approaches cooperative business by harkening back to the concept of "gentlemanly" conduct. Relationship building and cooperation has contributed to the success of his company: "when your back's against the wall in any industry you fall back on the relationships that you have built with people. You can't do that if you've just screwed them on price, for example. That's just not the way we do things."[21]

Second, try sending a referral for a client that you cannot take care of yourself to a friendly competitor. The competitor, after picking themselves up off the ground where they fell from surprise, will feel tremendously good about themselves, and about you. The savvy professional knows that the Power of Reciprocity kicks in and the competitor is correspondingly more likely to refer complementary business your way in the future. The vice president of Forrester Research Inc., Navi Radjou, captured this sentiment well when he said, "The traditional model says you have a fixed-size pie and you kill each other for a slice of it. This new vision calls for collaboration to increase the size of the pie."[22]

To put this in motion, consider your top rivals and give some thought to who they really are. What are their agendas? Think beyond the obvious and probe into what their real, deeper-meaning goals are. Sometimes, you'll be surprised at what you find. Then figure out what you can do to help them, in such a way that, of course, will not negatively impact you or your business. Actively offer your assistance and find ways to do good turns for them.

Third, be sure to acknowledge the value of your competitors. Complimenting and appreciating your competitors builds bridges, and you never know when bridges will be needed. Even the most sophisticated of forecasting models and strategic planning cannot predict just who your future collaborators will be. Often they are your stiffest competitors, people you simply disagree with or do not really like. Even your arch rival.

All smart politicians who last beyond one term quickly learn the power of respecting and connecting with their rivals. A politician, even at the upper reaches of the political hierarchy, needs the votes of her party, the other party or parties, voters, and the business and community leaders who lobby and support with resources and the weight of collective voices. Failing to cooperate will result in significantly hampered capability to get things done and can cripple a politician.

When your developer colleague is adamantly opposed to your insistence on environmental protections in the building of a new Super Wal-Mart in your area, the debate can be bitter. Her livelihood and philosophy of rapid economic growth directly and substantively clashes with your interest in protecting the environment you and your children live in. Her live-for-the-day approach is diametrically opposed to your "seventh generation" approach that looks at the results of today's actions on the environment of the future. When the debate airs in public, remember to recognize her for her business savvy and high-quality building projects. Then make your points as cogently and as convincingly as possible. Thank your colleague for her opinions, and let the chips fall where they may.

When you treat with respect those with whom you disagree with or compete, you not only act honorably, you also connect and create the foundation for a relationship that ultimately pays off. If you lose this battle, and the Super Wal-Mart is built without the environmental safeguards in place, you nevertheless developed kindness capital through your respectful conduct and established a bridge with your colleague. Next month, she could become your closest ally. This time the topic is whether to support legislation making it more difficult to use eminent domain that allows government to take dilapidated plots of land from private owners for the public good, like building parks or new residential and retail developments in blighted areas. Joining forces on this particular vote, you both reach out to your constituents—she to her fellow developers, and you to your environmentally minded allies hoping for more green space—and sway the vote in opposition to the measure.

Consider the benefit of building a "team of rivals," like President Abraham Lincoln did after his upset election victory in 1860. Known for extraordinary empathy-ability, Lincoln did not isolate and marginalize his failed opponents. Instead, he created what is described as the most unusual cabinet in history by assigning them to key posts, surrounding himself with his most arch rivals by appointing them to important positions in his government. Keeping his rivals close, getting to know them, and showing respect, ultimately won them over and created allies where only enemies had existed before. This bold move was credited with much of the success of the Lincoln era, including defeating the Confederates.[23]

With cooperation and kindness you ultimately win the war.

Short-Circuit Prisoner's Dilemma

It is positive to want to go first, provided the intention is to pave the way for others. Competition is negative when we wish to defeat others, to bring them down in order to lift ourselves up.

—Tensin Gyatso, the 14th Dalai Lama

I have experienced cooperation in action many times in both my legal and political careers. But never so dramatically as during a national conference for senior legislative staff when we were treated to a workshop with prominent NYU professor Allen J. Zerkin. With no preamble, he launched into an exercise in which we were grouped into two large clusters. We were told that the objective of the exercise was to do as well for ourselves as we could.

Each player had the option of raising either an X or a Y card when each round of the game was called. Holding up an X card could win a large number of points, but at a cost. Anyone else in the cluster who played a Y at the same time would lose a point. And, if more than one player went with an X, then everyone in the cluster would lose a point. However, if everyone chose Y, then all players would earn one point each.

When the first round was called, the cluster across the table from me immediately began an intense competition for points. Playing Xs furiously, they alternately racked up points and then lost them as their fellow players retaliated with their own Xs.

Our entire cluster played Ys each and every round and scored one point per player each time. We cooperated, agreeing to forgo the big, quick X rewards.

Our cluster had a ball. We had fun, worked together, and built relationships—all things that we felt brought us closer to the stated goal of "doing as well for ourselves as we could." We exchanged business cards, made plans for dinner that evening, and talked about how our cities from different regions of the nation could share best practices.

By the conclusion of the game the other cluster, on the contrary, needed therapy. One player said that she felt compelled to compete when other players used their Xs because, "If you're going to get got, you might as well do some getting."

Most importantly, when the points were tallied up, each player in our cluster did better than even the most skillful, competitive, and determined player from the other cluster. And, our cluster racked up many more points cumulatively than their cluster, weighed down with penalties and lost points.

Yes, we won.

We had spontaneously proven a key tenet of Robert Alexrod's axiomatic research that proved that not only is cooperation a friendlier business strategy, it is also the more successful one. Cooperating and seeking *mutual* benefit is not only the nice approach, it is the smart way to succeed. Axelrod, a University of Michigan political scientist, originated a tremendous body of research, coined the Prisoner's Dilemma after his original research involving hypothetical interrogations of prisoners and their decision-making process over whether to rat out their fellow inmate or not given different scenarios or potential gain or loss. Popularized by Axelrod's *The Evolution of Cooperation*, the Prisoner's

Dilemma findings have become synonymous with the benefits of cooperative behavior.

Axelrod took his original research and used game theory to allow for testing over time. Game theory studies and analyzes phenomenon—using computer modeling and mathematics—and has the advantage of real-world analysis as it looks at how players interact with each other and adapt their choices in relation to the choices of those they play with, or against.

Axelrod organized a computer tournament in the 1970s to apply the Prisoner's Dilemma theory. Computer scientists and programmers designed computer programs with different strategies to see which would achieve the most successful outcomes. The initial tournament provided for 200 rounds, allowing the participating computer programs to assess each others' past dealings. History and reputation was developed between the competing computer programs.

One of the competitors in Axelrod's tournament designed "Tit-for-tat," a simple computer program that played a deceptively simple strategy. The program would act cooperatively on the first round of the game, regardless of what the other player did or might do. Thereafter, it would mimic whatever the other player did, whether cooperative or competitive. The program was so simple, lacking the complex algorithms and strategic thinking that the others had devised, that its opponent could easily figure out what it was doing. If their program acted cooperatively, Tit-for-tat would too. If their program went for the throat, Tit-for-tat would do that too. The simplicity "guided" the opponent to the inevitable conclusion that to cooperate with it was its best strategy. The mirroring of the other players' actions tended to cause them to adapt and respond "in kind" as well. Tit-for-tat won that competition, as well as the many that came after it as astonished players looked for rematches.

The Tit-for-tat version of the Prisoner's Dilemma tells us that the ultimate strategy in a business relationship is to always start out by cooperating. Assume goodwill and good intentions, even if the short-term gains might seem temptingly larger if competing. To get the best result, the smartest thing one can do is to be kind and cooperative with ones' "opponent," who will in turn reciprocate that approach right back. Then, simply copy the other person. If he cooperates back, you work alongside each other gathering up mutual benefits as you go. When your cooperative behavior is reciprocated, as it often is, the highest "points" possible result. Persistent kindness reliably brings about cooperative win-wins and creates a positive environment for everyone concerned.

The real world works in the same way. You scratch my back, I'll scratch yours. This tit-for-tat response enables competing interests to be resolved with positive, win-win outcomes—if both parties are willing to play nice.

What if both parties aren't willing to play nice?

Fuel to the Fire

If the world seems cold, then perhaps it is time to pause and uncover the role that we have each played in lowering the temperature.

—Harvey Hornstein, social scientist and author

Tit-for-tat actually means "equivalent retaliation." It can be positive (as we've already examined) or negative in the "right back at ya" fashion. Negative action or intention is often met by, or leads to, another negative action or intention.

In the Prisoner's Dilemma experiments, when the Tit-for-tat player was met with uncooperative behavior, it would retaliate. In real-life application, should the other party choose to compete or backstab, you may be forced to "retaliate" with a less cooperative or outright competitive move of your own. Remember, nice is not a pushover strategy. Standing strong or failing to cooperate in response to an aggressive move of another should be enough to guide them back toward cooperation.

However, be wary of causing an escalation of negative behavior. The end result of a spiral of negative tit-for-tat behavior is the much feared "lose-lose" outcome bringing to light the classic saying: *"An eye for an eye makes the whole world blind."* The Tit-for-tat program showed that it is important to be willing to step out and cooperate again to break a negative cycle. Although it would mimic the behavior of its competitor, it was also programmed to randomly throw in another cooperative gesture. We have that choice in our professional lives too—to pull out of a competitive situation and essentially "reset" the relationship.

In addition to the world of computer modeling, the natural world has much to tell us about why cooperation is the more successful approach.

Natural Selection

No one can fail to reap the advantage of a proper, courteous and likable approach, or fail to be handicapped by an improper, offensive and resented one.

—Emily Post

Much like natural selection in biology weeds out non-adaptive physical features in nature, non-niceness tends to be punished or weeded out in business. Oddly enough, the vampire bat is a good analogy of how cooperation works and taking advantage fails. The vampire bat typically lives in colonies, though it hunts alone. When a bat gets a meal of blood, it will often feed some of that regurgitated blood to bats that weren't able to secure their own meals during that particular hunt. Vampire bats aren't doing this because they are particularly kind. Rather, they are lining up potential meal donors for themselves, should they need a borrowed meal in the future.

The real catch here is that any bat that receives a "free" meal from another bat, but then fails to reciprocate with its own donated meal at a later date, is punished. These non-reciprocating bats are actually remembered by the other bats, and if they fail to reciprocate often enough, they are ultimately kicked out of the colony. The free-riding bat, therefore, fails to pass its genes, and non-nice tendencies, to offspring.

Business has some resemblance to the bat colony. In business, there is always a risk of coming up against an unscrupulous, zero-sum-style competitor or company that attacks you. But cheaters and non-reciprocators are not tolerated, at least not often and not for long. Natural selection in business means that individuals and companies that provide good products and services are chosen time and again for repeat business. However, companies that cut corners or fail to meet obligations are not revisited, ultimately "weeding them out"—out of business, that is.

Thus, being cutthroat and calculating is a highly *unsuccessful* strategy, particularly in the mid- to long-term. We've already seen how non-niceness doesn't work, as customers and employees make alternative choices when treated poorly. Cheaters and opportunists are ferreted out, moving the non-nice further and further from their goals.

Sure we all can name a classic "mean" boss who succeeded. These examples do exist, but by their very noteworthiness and rareness prove the limits of their success. If a mean boss who seems to be successful comes to mind, try following her career over the course of time. Typically the non-nice have short-run successes, not sustained by lasting relationships and respect that allow for long-term accomplishments. A one-deal wonder can make a great business move and obtain a big payoff by stepping on others, but they won't be able to do it again.

This leads to a tremendously exciting chain of inquiry and reflection of how our own behavior influences our circumstances, be they of wealth or misery. Instead of benefiting from a caring reputation, positive paybacks, and the other Powers, could you be attracting negative results to you? As Professor Harvey Hornstein stated: "As the chain of social encounters turns full circle, every encounter is influenced by preceding ones and we are each potentially the remote victims of our own misdeeds."[24] Give it some thought.

In spite of the unconstructiveness of competitive practices, those in positions of power seem especially susceptible to its allure.

Power Play

Unfortunately for many people, having power is like drinking salt water. The more you drink, the thirstier you get.

—John Maxwell

Power is a dangerous commodity if not handled with extreme care. Those who seek power in order to do good must guard carefully against the exploitation of that power once they attain it. Most people in positions of power got there by a combination of motivation, smarts, and genuine interest in creating some good. Many politicians enter into the political fray to represent constituents' interests and make positive changes. Business people typically want to create a product that is currently lacking in the marketplace, and that can add value to society.

Power can be an intoxicating distorter of priorities and values. The thirst for power can overtake the original purpose of obtaining the power. Power tends to perpetuate itself as those in the seat of power struggle to retain and expand their reach.

Heightened by the seeming freedom from the regular checks and balances that great power and money can bring, some people falter, and falter badly, bringing to mind the words of Abraham Lincoln that "Nearly all men can stand adversity, but if you want to test a man's character, give him power." The multibillion-dollar corporate frauds perpetrated by Enron, Tyco, Arthur Andersen, WorldCom, HealthSouth, and Adelphia were brought about, in large part, by CEOs who seemed to feel that their money and power insulated them from the governing legal and ethical boundaries. Harry Truman advised that "If a man can accept a situation in a place of power with the thought that it's only temporary, he comes out all right. But when he thinks he is the cause of the power, that can be his ruination." When maintaining and growing power becomes the central focus, then everyone seems to be a potential source of competition. It can result in increased stereotyping and aggression, and correspondingly less niceness and cooperative behavior.

Fortunately, the deeply ingrained competitive tendencies of North American culture can be short circuited—person by person, one business and industry at a time—with the Power of Connecting:

Practice Pointers

A competitive culture endures by tearing people down.
> —Jules Henry, professor, American anthropologist, and sociologist

With all the benefits of connecting and networking, you'll want to immediately put the Power of Connecting into practice:

-   Reconnect with someone with whom you have lost touch. Think of a client who used to send you business but then stopped a couple of years ago. Find out something he or she is interested in and send them a note in the mail with a relevant article attached.

- Create a "marina-like" environment in your workplace setting. Emphasize helpfulness and make some element of your environment extraordinary.

- Solicit others' opinions and really *listen* to their advice.

- Take note of what your coworkers' hobbies are and then acknowledge them—that is, bring in a small token from the baseball game.

- Call a colleague and leave a brief voice message just to touch base and to share something positive you were thinking about him or her. Be specific in the message. Explain how you were reminded of how organized he or she was on the last project you worked on together. Have no more agenda than that.

- Think of a business contact with whom you have a poor relationship and find a way to contact him or her in a positive way. You might want to apologize, if needed, or just start a new dialogue.

- Take the focus off your own personal or professional drama, even if just for the day. Pull your thoughts away from you, from how you look/sound/appear and force yourself to think about how you can get to know and connect with someone today.

- Build a professional association network. Many professions have associations already: if yours doesn't, be the one to send out an e-mail invitation to others like you and host a meeting or event to get to know others.

- E-mail or write notes to people to get to know them and to cement business acquaintanceships.

- Use daily reminders to keep you focused on cooperation rather than competition. Print and post inspirational sayings around your work space, or have your PDA beep you with cooperative reminders from time to time.

- Have a cooperation buddy. When you are feeling competitive, or just irritated, run a thorny issue by him or her so he or she can remind you to focus on *mutual* benefit.

- Whenever you feel competitive, ask yourself "is this kind?" This simple question, if taken seriously, will cause you to pause, reflect, and avoid lashing out.

- "Retaliate" a negative act toward you with a positive one of your own to break the cycle.

- Acknowledge the good ideas and good deeds of your competitors.

Now that you have the Five Powers of Kindness in hand, and you are reaping the amazing results of your flourishing kindness capital, it is the perfect time to take the next step—from success to significance.

Chapter 7

From Success to Significance

Real joy comes not from ease or riches or from the praise of men, but from doing something worthwhile.

—Wildred T. Grenfell, philanthropist

When Mayor Loveridge was exploring a theme for his 2005 State of the City Address, he wanted to emphasize that the markers of success were already in place for the City of Riverside. This Southern California city of more than 300,000 people, the 61st largest city in the United States, has all the metropolitan amenities you might expect, including an enviable Southern California climate and a location that takes advantage of near proximity to both mountains and beaches. It has been judged a success by many associations—receiving state and national awards for its information technologies, environmental innovations, and economic development techniques. It is already, he stressed, a successful city. Knowing he would be delivering this speech to a thousand or so civic leaders and setting the course for the up-coming year, Mayor Loveridge wanted to do more than recount the many successes and remaining challenges.

When success is already secured, what then? As we bantered back and forth, we acknowledged that what is not a guaranteed corollary of *success* is actual *significance*. Significance is something else, something qualitatively, rather than quantitatively, different from success.

Significance does not mean simply having *more* success. While success could mean having everything you want, significance is being all that you can be. It is about making a positive difference, leaving a legacy—a deeper, meaningful impact. If you, like me, want your lasting legacy to be more than leaving behind a fancy car or house or two, then you need to adopt a purposeful mission. Academic, writer, and humorist Leo Rosten captured the meaning of significance when he said, "I cannot believe that the purpose of life is to be happy. I think the purpose of life is to be useful, to be responsible, to be compassionate. It is, above all, to matter, to count, to stand for something, to have made some difference that you lived at all." The dash demarcating the beginning year of your life and the date of your death is small. Yet the space it signifies in between encapsulates the whole sum of your life, the contribution you make.

As for Mayor Loveridge, he entitled his speech "From Success to Significance." He touched on the common markers of municipal success in the speech—economic development signified by good stores and restaurants, and standard of living measures—but he also focused on another level, that of lasting impact. He explored concepts such as social capital and an active and engaged community, linking the communities of faith, creating true diversity and respect, and leaving a legacy for future residents.

The mayor also later sought and won office as an officer and future president of the National League of Cities, a national organization representing some 19,000 cities and towns across the United States. In that role, he will be able to contribute to the rebuilding of America's municipal infrastructure in the years to come.

Exploring kindness capital throughout these chapters, you may already have uncovered, or rediscovered, what is truly significant to you, and what you want your dash to mean. We've already seen that kindness is the ultimate *business* tool. Kindness is also the ultimate *life* tool. It may seem a little simplistic at first for a 21st-century business book, but making kindness your credo will create both the prosperity *and* the significance you seek.

Kindness guides you through your whole life and provides you with a blueprint for significance. And you must have a blueprint if you are to achieve significance. Not many people do. When you choose to develop kindness capital, you ensure that whatever you do at work, whatever you do with your family, and whatever you do with your passions is done with kindness and an intent to help others. You simply make being kind guide your actions. You do not have to be a saint to be kind.

My last practice pointer for creating both success and significance is a simple step. Create a Capitalizing on Kindness Charter. The Kindness Charter will remind you about the Five Powers of

Kindness and guide you and your company (if you have one), toward making the most positive impact that you can. Use the one at the back of this book or go to my Website, *www.kindnesscapital.com*, to customize one that suits you and your company, and to print out the other paractice pointers.

Moving from a success to a significance mindset is indeed a shift in focus. Perhaps you will find it easier when you recognize that the pursuit of material success has inherent downfalls and dangers.

Pass Up the Pursuit

Often people attempt to live their lives backwards: they try to have more things, or more money, in order to do more of what they want so that they will be happier.

—Margaret Young, entertainer

There can be too much of a good thing. When materialistic success is too hard sought, happiness and satisfaction actually decrease. Individuals whose goals center around money and other superficial indicators of success report less satisfaction or happiness in their lives. [1] Research indicates that many of those with abundant material wealth are actually *less* happy than the rest of us. They experience more depression, anxiety, and less pleasant emotions.

They are probably suffering from the social plague, termed "affluenza" in the 1950s, resulting from relentlessly pursuing the "good life." Social scientist John de Graaf calls it: "… a painful, contagious, socially transmitted condition of overload, debt, anxiety, and waste resulting from the dogged pursuit of more."[2]

Similarly coined the "hedonic treadmill" in 1975 by psychologists Philip Brickman and Donald Campbell, the pursuit of material satisfaction tends to be both insatiable and ultimately unsatisfying. Once we have our "dream home," isn't it tempting to start thinking of a new home, one that is even bigger and better? Don't we tend to look with envy at the neighbor's new convertible, even as we drive our new car into the garage? With each material gain we become accustomed to a new level of materialism and seek out more and more things to give us the momentary psychological boost that money *can* buy. When on the hedonic treadmill, "our brains do not recognize an absolute level of satisfaction. In other words, no matter how much we have, we want more."[3]

Sure, acquiring new commodities and "stuff" might make you feel good in the moment. But such feelings of well-being are transient. As soon as we adjust to that new level of affluence, we are hit with a sense of lack and dissatisfaction that sends us back on to the treadmill of wealth accumulation. Stress, overwork, and less sleep are just some of the consequences of affluenza and the hedonic treadmill. Chronically caught up in the allure of materialism, the relationships, healthy successes, and significance that money *cannot* buy, to suffer.

The trend toward materialism affects more than just the individual. It impacts whole nations. While the wealth of the United States and England has grown during the past half-century (the United States is four times wealthier in 2008 than it was in 1950), measures of psychological well-being have not grown. People in the United States and other developed countries report being no

happier, or slightly less happy, now than they were in less economically fruitful times.[4] In Japan, in spite of a fivefold increase
in real income, happiness has actually declined during the past 50
years. One explanation is that our increasingly materialistic society influences us to spend the increased wealth on ourselves,
throwing us handily onto the treadmill.

Instead, focusing on kindness, happiness, and building significance is a key way to reverse the trend toward materialism. A
small number of governments are wising up to the importance
of understanding these factors. The government of Bhutan, a
tiny, relatively poor country in the eastern Himalayas, is looking
at measuring "Gross National Happiness" to assess and encourage citizen satisfaction. Gross National Happiness and other in-
dices track parallel to the traditional measure of gross domestic
product (GDP), which look at the products and monetary gains
produced by a nation. Thailand established a Gross Domestic
Happiness Index that measures contentment on a 1 to 10 scale.
Unsurprisingly, Thais report less happiness at times when political turmoil and sectarian violence have flared up, and their political situation complicates such an assessment.

Developed countries too, from the U.K. to Australia, show
they are cognizant of the effect of happiness on the health of a
nation by their happiness indexes. A U.S. organization, Redefining Progress, has developed a measure called the Genuine Progress
Indicator (GPI) to attempt to remedy the reliance on the exchange of money and products as the sole measure of the success
of the nation. The GPI starts with some of the same economic

data as the GDP, but then diverges significantly by taking socially responsible, social capital-building criteria into account. It adds the value of volunteerism and housework to the equation and subtracts the costs of crime and natural resource depletion to come up with a more balanced measure of how well the nation is doing. Taking the GPI as a point of analysis, while the economy has been, more or less, steadily increasing since 1950, the overall health and well-being of the nation peaked in the 1970s, and has stagnated since then.[5]

In fact, research indicates that people are made happier when they give away money to others, rather than keeping it for themselves. Assuming the basic bills are paid, getting more money, hoarding what we have, or simply spending it on ourselves seems to do nothing to increase our level of happiness. On the contrary, people report feeling significantly happier when they donate at least a portion of windfall monies to others.[6]

I'm certainly not suggesting that you cease striving for financial success, promotions, or prominence and start giving away all of your belongings. The trappings of success can make us feel good. They can also help us achieve significance by putting us in a better position to make a difference. But the evidence suggests tempering the search for material benefits with the search for living a "good life" over a materialist "goods life."

Let's dispense with one final kindness inhibitor that might seem to stand between you and the success *and* significance you so richly deserve.

Kindness Inhibitor: *Expectations*

Act with kindness, but do not expect gratitude.

—Confuscious

Nice people genuinely care about others—other people's feelings, concerns, and interests register daily on their radar range. The truly kind among us are nice to everyone they encounter simply for the sake of kindness, without expectation of payoff. From acts as simple as smiling at a customer to improve a mood, choosing to collaborate with a competitor, and holding the door open for a companion, the nice person is not playing the "tit-for-tat" game in anticipation of payback or benefits.

When you do something nice in business, the gratification can be delayed or absent altogether. Building a company using kindness to employees, respect of competitors, and the desire to build a business that contributes something to the overall good of society, takes some time, effort, and patience. This is where the final kindness inhibitor can rear its ugly head—the expectation of gratitude and results can put a damper on the desire to be kind.

Sure, it is nice to be acknowledged, but the purpose of kindness must always primarily be kindness. The most liberating and honorable reason to be kind is because it is the right thing to do. Mark Twain wryly suggested that we should "Always do right. This will gratify some people, and astonish the rest." When it becomes an expectation, then people begin to be discouraged if they feel they are not being appreciated enough. We can become parsimonious with our kindness because we anticipate or expect to be thanked by others.

A more difficult barrier still is when we face ingratitude or resentment. Sometimes the people we help and direct our kindness to are not interested in or even willing to receive that kindness. Not everyone will graciously accept the nice person's kindness and return the favor. Sometimes, they might be unappreciative or, even worse, unkind to you anyway.

But kindness is not a relative mandate. Even if someone treats you with disdain or even with cruelty, you must abide by the rule that is golden. Respond with compassion when treated with coldness, be patient even when others are abrupt. Especially tricky is responding kindly to a slight or insult when your instinct tells you to respond "in kind" with a sharp comment or undermining move.

Being a nice guy or gal will not inoculate you against unkindness or injustice. Sometimes, you might *actually* get taken advantage of because your efforts to be kind put you in a position of extending yourself and making you more vulnerable. It is worth the risk. You will have lost little but safeguarded much: "The day we stop helping one another in order to guarantee not being taken advantage of is the day that evil wins. Of course our kindness will keep cons and cheats in business, but we can live with that. When our motives are pure, we should be able to live with the embarrassment of being played for a fool. What we can't accept is a society where caring and compassion shrivel under our suspicions."[7]

Most people you encounter are dealing with some trying situation, deep-seated issues, remorse, or ill will. Recognizing that the person who is treating you poorly is likely experiencing hardship in his or her life can help you to show the compassion that recognizes that person's intrinsic value. There is no more challenging yet rewarding feeling than taking the high road when faced with those who do not.

Fortunately, when we find we don't like what we see around us—in our personal or professional lives—we have the option of recreating that space through our acts of kindness. Without taking responsibility, we can't realistically "hope" for the world to somehow develop positively. If you are capable of doing good within your neighborhood, country, and beyond, then you must. "The only way to ensure that kindness lives on your planet is to put it there yourself," said Robert J. Furey, author of *The Joy of Kindness*.

If you are not acting as the example, building kindness capital wherever you go and with whatever you do, then who is and who will?

"As If"

Every man must decide whether he will walk in the light of creative altruism or the darkness of destructive selfishness. This is the judgment. Life's most persistent and urgent question is, what are you doing for others?

—Dr. Martin Luther King, Jr.

Kindness has a more profound impact on others than the giving of advice, donations, time, or intellect. Kindness allows you to tap into your true potential and enlivens the potential of others. Kindness can make and remake your professional life, your best self, and indeed the very world around you.

Fortunately there are "giants" among us who model the way of kindness capital. Individuals and corporations—from local to famous—examined throughout this book have built kindness capital for vibrantly successful and significant lives. We learn from them and they boost us to heights we might otherwise not reach. In the words of Sr. Isaac Newton, we "Stand on the shoulders of giants." You have met many of them in this book.

While you and I may not be in the position that some of these "giants" we looked at are, we *do* have the power to act locally and individually to create significance hand-in-hand with success.

Greater acknowledgment of the immense value of kindness in creating both professional success and significance is evident in a trend in higher education across America. Business schools are increasingly offering M.B.A. programs with classes that address ethics, spirituality, and personal fulfillment in the workplace.

Professors in such courses have considerable flexibility to create coursework that stimulates their students' capacity and awareness of doing good, and to integrate it early into their professional lives. Professor Rao at Columbia University, developed the "as if" exercise. In the "as if" exercise, business students are required to totally immerse themselves in an alternate reality; for example, treating every single person they meet as if it were that person's last day on Earth. In this exercise, students "pretend" that others' time is of utmost importance and preciousness because it is so marked. The students are faced with developing ways to treat these individuals with the utmost in kindness and helpfulness. Professor Rao deserves kudos for his creativity.

How about we stop "pretending" that kindness is only relevant when time is short? Why not take every opportunity to become the very best we can be? Rather than passively offering kindnesses when convenient, seek out opportunities to spread generous acts and deeds to make a difference, to create significance in both your professional, and personal, life. I have heard kindness described as the currency of our hearts. When you intentionally and consciously spread kindness, you'll find that there is plenty of "gold" in your future, and the futures of those you touch.

Capitalizing on Kindness Charter for Success and Significance

Power of Reputation

I will build a caring reputation by actively keeping the best interests of others in mind.

It will give employees and customers the courtesy and best service they deserve and gain their loyalty and best effort.

Power of Reciprocity

I will build reciprocity points by doing favors for others and paying-forward to everyone I encounter.

It will help others and result in favors being done for me.

Power of Personality

I will develop my likeable, positive personality.

It will make others feel good and gain their support.

Power of Thanks

I will thank and appreciate everyone in my personal and professional life.

It will meet their deep-seated need for acknowledgement and gain tremendous loyalty and appreciation in return.

Power of Connecting

I will develop empathy and a strong network.

It will help others achieve their goals and put me in a position to be their preferred business partner.

Creating Signficance

I will actively build kindness capital and determine what my significant contribution will be.

It will be my legacy.

NOTES

Chapter 1: Kindness Capital

1. Tad Tuleja, *Beyond the Bottom Line: How Business Leaders are Turning Principles into Profits* (New York: Facts on File, 1985), 196. Between 1952 and 1982 the GNP of the U.S. increased just 2.5 times while the net income of the socially responsible companies grew 23 times.

2. Ibid, 197.

3. Thomas J. Peters and Robert H. Waterman Jr., *In Search of Excellence: Lessons from America's Best-Run Companies* (New York: Harper & Row, 1982), 11.

4. Landry, Craig E. et al., "Toward an Understanding of the Economics of Charity: Evidence from a Field Experiment," *Quarterly Journal of Economics* 121, no.2 (2006): 747–82.

5. Jim Collins, *Good to Great* (New York: HarperCollins, 2001) 1.

6. Gallup Poll, July 24-27, 2006, based on randomly drawn telephone interviews with 1,001 U.S. adults.

7. Tony Robbins, *Unlimited Power: The New Science of Personal Achievement* (New York: Simon & Schuster, 1986) 5. Emphasis mine.

Chapter 2: The Power of Reputation

1. Charisse Jones and Andrea Stone, "Reports: Spitzer Resignation Imminent," *USA Today*, March 12, 2008, 5A.

2. Barna Research Online, "Americans Speak: Enron, WorldCom and Others Are Result of Inadequate Moral Training by Families," July 22, 2002, *www.barna.org*. Survey consisted of a nationwide random sample of 1,012 adults.

3. HarrisInteractive, "The Harris Poll #4," January 13, 2005, *www.harrisinteractive.com/harris_poll*. Survey consisted of a nationwide cross section of 2,092 adults in the U.S.

4. Watson Wyatt, "Watson Wyatt WorkUSA 2006/ 2007" survey, *www.watsonwyatt.com*. Survey was conducted of more than 12,000 full-time U.S. workers across all job levels and major industries.

5. John C. Maxwell, *Ethics 101: What Every Leader Needs to Know* (New York: Time Warner Book Group, 2003) 16–18. Maxwell and other authors have summarized research on the many religions and cultures that have a principle much like the Golden Rule, from Confucianism to Islam. In that sense, the golden rule principle is the closest thing to a universal rule of behavior that exists.

6. Ibid, 26–27

7. J.C. Penney, *Fifty Years with the Golden Rule* (New York: Harper and Brothers, 1950) 56.

8. Michael Josephson, *The Best is Yet to Come: More Thoughts on Being a Better Person and Living a Better Life*, 66.

9. Maxwell, *Ethics 101,* 100.

10. White House Office of Consumer Affairs, 1985 survey, as reported by the Research Institute of America.

11. Paul C. Judge, "EMC Corp." *Fast Company* (June 2001), 11.

12. Meladee McCarty and Hanoch McCarty, *Acts of Kindness: How to Create a Kindness Revolution* (Deerfield Beach: Health Communications Inc, 1994), 81.

13. Jessica Guynn, "Amazon's net doubles in the 4th quarter," *LA Times*, January 21, 2008, C3, quoting Tim Boyd, analyst with American Technology Research.

14. Robert Half International Inc. "2008 Salary Guide," 3. Survey consisted of 1,400 Chief Financial Officers.

15. Ranjay Gulati, Sarah Huffman, and Gary Neilson, "The Barista Principle—Starbucks and the Rise of Relational Capital," *Strategy+Business*, 2002, referencing Howard Schultz' 1997 memoir, *Pour Your Heart Into It*.

16. Arthur C. Brooks, *Who Really Cares: The Surprising Truth about Compassionate Conservatism* (Cambridge Massachusetts: Basic Books, 2006).

17. Steve Hamm, "Competition Edition," *BusinessWeek*, Aug 21, 2006, 93.

18. Steven L. Adler, *BusinessWeek*, March 3, 2008, 3 and 6.

19. Meladee McCarty and Hanoch McCarty, *Acts of Kindness: How to Create a Kindness Revolution* (Deerfield Beach: Health Communications Inc., 1994), 86.

Chapter 3: The Power of Reciprocity

1. Francis Flynn, "The relative impact of perceived imbalance and frequency on favor exchange among employees: Tradeoffs between social status and productivity" (paper presented at the Organizational Behavior Colloquium Series, Kellogg Graduate School of Business, Northwestern University, October, 2002). Study was conducted of 161 engineers.

2. Ibid, 133.

3. Harvey A. Hornstein, *Cruelty & Kindness: A New Look at Aggression and Altruism* (New Jersey: Prentice-Hall Inc, 1976), 133

4. Allan Luks and Peggy Payne, *The Healing Power of Doing Good: The Health and Spiritual Benefits of Helping Others* (Fawcett Columbine, 1991) 17.

5. Jonathan Van Meter, "The Producer," *Vogue*, March 2005.

6. Pierre de Coubertin, "The Olympic Creed" inspired by Bishop Ethelbert Talbot, speech, Olympic Games 1908.

7. Bryson, Kelly, *Don't Be Nice, Be Real: Balancing Compassion for Self with Compassion for Others* (Santa Rosa: Author's Publishing Cooperative, 2002), 15.

8. Daniel Goleman, *Primal Leadership: Learning to Lead with Emotional Intelligence.* (Boston, Massachusetts Harvard Business School Press, 2002), 65.

9. Lois Frankel, *Nice Girls Don't Get the Corner Office: 101 Unconscious Mistakes Women Make That Sabatoge Their Careers*. (New York: Warner Business Books. 2004), 87–88.

Chapter 4: The Power of Personality

1. Jim Collins, *Good to Great* (New York: HarperBusiness, 2001). For a fuller examination of the liability of an overly charismatic CEO.

2. Gladwell, Malcolm. *The Tipping Point: How Little Things Can Make a Big Difference* (New York: Back Bay Books, 2000, 2002), 84–85.

3. Meladee McCarty and Hanoch McCarty, *Acts of Kindness: How to Create a Kindness Revolution* (Deerfield Beach: Health Communications Inc, 1994), 112.

4. Michael Josephson, "Character Counts" e-newsletter, Dec 16-22, 2005. *www.michaeljosephson.com.*

5. Martin E.P. Seligman, *Learned Optimism: How to Change Your Mind and Your Life* (New York: Pocket Books, 1990, 1998), 256.

6. Chip Health and Dan Health, "Leadership is a Muscle," *Fast Company*, Issue 117, July 2007, 62.

7. Alice M. Isen, "Positive Affect," in *Handbook of Cognition and Emotion*, eds. Tim Dalgleish and Mick J. Power, (Chichester, England: Wiley, 1999).

8. Robert A. Emmons, *Thanks!: How the new science of gratitude can make you happier* (New York: Houghton Mifflin, 2007), 13.

9. Tom Rath and Donald O. Clifton, *How Full is Your Bucket?* (New York: Gallup Press, 2004), 47.

10. Ibid. Interaction ratios of 3 positive to 1 negative resulted in increased productivity, and 5 positive interactions for every 1 negative was found to be ideal according to Rath and Clifton citing Losada, M. "The complex dynamics of high performance teams," *Mathematical and Computer Modeling* 30,(1999): 189–192.

11. Seligman, *Learned Optimism,* 256.

12. Tim Sanders, *The Likeability Factor: How to Boost Your L-Factor & Achieve Your Life's Dreams* (New York: Crown Publishers, 2005), 35.

13. Melinda Tamkins (research presented at the American Psychological Society's conference, Toronto, Ontario, Canada, June 18, 2001).

14. Jack Mitchell. *Hug Your People: The Proven Way to Hire, Inspire, and Recognize Your Employees and Achieve Remarkable Results* (New York: Hyperion Books, 2008), 14.

15. William S. Cottringer, "Nice Guys Finish First," *Security Management,* 44, no. 6 (2000): 24.

16. Katsuhiko Eguchi, "The Importance of Being Amiable," *Japan Close-Up* (2004): 42.

17. Linda Kaplan Thaler and Robin Koval, *The Power of Nice: How to Conquer the Business World with Kindness* (New York: Doubleday, 2006), 3.

18. Bert Decker. *You've Got to Be Believed to Be Heard: Reach the First Brain to Communicate in Business and in Life* (New York: St. Martin's Press USA, 1992).

19. Sanders, *The Likeability Factor,* 31

20. James E. Challenger, "The Job Hunt: Land a New Job? Here is How to Keep It," November 13, 2007, 4.

21. Jenni Laidman, "Making an Impression" *The Topeka Capital-Journal,* June 25, 2001. According to research conducted by Frank Bernieri and Tricia Prickett, University of Toledo in Ohio.

22. James D. Laird, "Self-Attribution of Emotion: The Effects of Expressive Behavior on the Quality of Emotional Experience" *Journal of Personality and Social Psychology.* 29:4 (1974) 480.

23. Daniel Goleman, *Primal Leadership: Learning to Lead with Emotional Intelligence* (Boston, Mass.: Harvard Business School Press, 2004), 10.

24. "America The Rude," *CBS News,* October 14, 2005, available at www.cbsnews.com, citing an Associated Press-Ipsos poll. And, P.M. Forni et al. "The Baltimore Workplace Civility Study," January 2003, 2.

Chapter 5: The Power of Thanks

1. Stephen M.R. Covey, *The Speed of Trust: The One Thing That Changes Everything* (New York: Free Press, 2006), 149–150.

2. Thomas J. Peters and Robert H. Waterman, *In Search of Excellence: Lessons from America's Best-Run Companies* (New York: Harper & Row, 1982), 55.

3. Robert Half International. "Robert Half WorkPlace Pulse 2007: Your Guide to Trends Impacting Today's Accounting and Finance Managers," 2007, 13.

4. Goleman, *Primal Leadership,* 83

5. Rath and Clifton, *How Full is Your Bucket?* 33.

6. Sharon McGowan, "Engaged Employees: Going the Extra Mile," Hudson, 2005, 10. Study found that a mere 14 percent of employees are engaged at mid to large size companies. And, Towers Perrin Consultancy, "Towers Perrin Global Workforce Study, Closing the Engagement Gap: A Road Map for Driving Superior Business Performance," 2007-2008, 4, found that 21 percent are engaged.

7. Towers Perrin Consultancy, "Towers Perrin Global Workforce Study, Closing the Engagement Gap: A Road Map for Driving Superior Business Performance," 2007-2008, 4. Study found that 38 percent of employees worldwide are partly to fully disengaged.

8. P.M. Fiorni, et al., "The Baltimore Workplace Civility Study," January 2003.

9. Rath and Clifton, *How Full is Your Bucket?* 33. This equals nearly 10 percent of the U.S. GDP.

10. Daniel Gross, *Forbes Greatest Business Stories of All Times* (New York: John Wiley & Sons, Inc.: 1996), 242.

11. Thomas J. Peters and Robert H. Waterman, *In Search of Excellence: Lessons from America's Best-Run Companies* (New York: Harper & Row, 1982), 58–59.

12. Ibid, 57.

13. A.M. Isen, "Success, Failure, Attention, and Reaction to Others: The Warm Glow of Success," *Journal of Personality and Social Psychology* 15, no.4 (1970) 294–301.

14. Keise Izuma, Daisuke Saito, and Norihiro Sadato, "Processing of Social and Monetary Rewards in the Human Striatum," *Neuron* 58, no. 2 (April 24, 2008) 284–294. Study consisted of 19 people using a brain imaging technique or fMRI.

15. Rath and Clifton, *How Full is Your Bucket?* 28.

16. Towers Perrin Consultancy, "Towers Perrin Global Workforce Study," 5.

17. Barbara Kiviat, "The Rage to Engage," *Time Magazine*, Thursday April 17, 2008, based on Tower Perrin Consultancy, "Towers Perrin Global Workforce Study, 5.

18. Barry Ray, "Who's afraid of the big bad boss? Plenty of us, new FSU study shows" *Florida State University News,* http://www.fsu.edu/news/2006/12/04/bad.boss/ study.

19. Robert A. Emmons, *Thanks!: How the new science of gratitude can make you happier* (New York: Houghton Mifflin Company, 2007), 139.

Chapter 6: The Power of Connecting

1. Captain Michael D. Abrashoff, *It's Your Ship: Management Techniques from the Best Damn Ship in the Navy* (New York: Warner Books Inc., 2002).

2. Peters and Waterman, *In Search of Excellence*, 55.

3. Olivia McIvor, *The Business of Kindness: Creating Work Environments Where People Thrive* (Lions Bay, B.C.: Fairwinds Press, 2006), 38.

4. Goleman, *Primal Leadership*, 50.

5. Jim Collins, *Good to Great* (New York: HarperCollins, 2001) 28.

6. Goleman, *Primal Leadership*, 60.

7. Towers Perrin Consultancy, 2007-2008 Towers Perrin Global Workforce Study, *www.towersperrin.com.*

8. Stephen M.R. Covey, *The Speed of Trust: The One Thing That Changes Everything* (New York: Free Press, 2006), 80.

9. Peters and Waterman, *In Search of Excellence*, 14.

10. Goleman, *Primal Leadership*, 50

11. Joseph A. Michell, *The Starbucks Experience: 5 Principles for Turning Ordinary into Extraordinary.* (New York: McGraw-Hill, 2007), 7

12. Mike Brewster and Frederick Dalzell, *Driving Change: The UPS Approach to Business* (New York: Hyperion, 2007), 24, 186.

13. Ronald M. Sharpiro and Mark A. Jankowski, with James Dale, *The Power of Nice: How to Negotiate so Everyone Wins-Especially You!* (New York: John Wiley & Sons Inc., 2001 revised edition), 49.

14. Robert D. Putnam, "E Pluribus Unum: Diversity and Community in the Twenty-first Century. The 2006 Johan Skytte Prize Lecture," *Scandinavian Political Studies* 30, no.2 (2007).

15. Associated Press, "Connections are his currency," *Los Angeles Times*, C3, January 21, 2008.

16. Mark Granovetter, *Getting a Job: A study of contacts and careers*, 2nd edition (Chicago: The University of Chicago Press. 1995), 22.

17. Accountemps press release "Thanks, But No Thanks", August 9, 2007, www.accountemps.com. Reporting on a national poll with responses from 150 senior executives in the nation's 1,000 largest firms.

18. Catherine Arnst, "Selfish Genes and Mellow Monkeys," *Business Week*, The Competition Edition, August 21/28, 2008, 59.

19. Peter Coy, ed., "The Poll", *Business Week*, The Competition Issue, August 21/28, 2006, 42–45.

20. Peter Coy, "Sleeping with the Enemy," The Competition Issue, August 21/28, 2006, 97.

21. William Drew, "Are Gentlemen a Dying Breed?" *The London Times*, May 20, 2008.

22. Coy, "Sleeping with the Enemy," *Business Week*, 96.

23. Doris Kearns Goodwin. *Team of Rivals: The Political Genius of Abraham Lincoln* (New York: Simon & Schuster. 2005).

24. Harvey Hornstein, *Cruelty and Kindness*, (New Jersey: Prentice-Hall Inc., 1976), 133

Chapter 7: From Success to Significance

1. Dr. Tim Kasser, "The High Price of Materialism: A Psychological Inquiry," *The MIT Press* (2002): 18.

2. John de Graaf, *Affluenza: The All-Consuming Epidemic* (San Francisco: Berrett-Koehler, 2001), 2.

3. Catherine Arnst, "Selfish Genes and Mellow Monkeys." *Business Week*, The Competition Edition, August 21/28, 2006, 59.

4. Elizabeth W. Dunn, Lara B. Aknin, and Michael I. Norton, "Spending Money on Others Promotes Happiness" *Science*, 5870 (2008) 3. And, David G. Myers, "The Funds, Friends, and Faith of Happy People." *American Psychologist*. 55 (2000).

5. Dr. John Talberth, Clifford Cobb, and Noah Slattery, "The Genuine Progress Indicator 2006: A Tool for Sustainable Development," February 2007, a report of Redefining Progress available electronically at *www.rprogress.org*.

6. Elizabeth W. Dunn, Lara B. Aknin, and Michael I. Norton, "Spending Money on Others Promotes Happiness" *Science* 5870 (2008) 4.

7. Michael Josephson, *The Best is Yet To Come*, 115.

BIBLIOGRAPHY

Abrashoff, Captain Michael D. *It's Your Ship: Management Techniques from the Best Damn Ship in the Navy.* New York: Warner Books Inc., 2002.

Barabasi, Albert-Laszlo. *Linked.* Cambridge, Mass.: Plume, 2003.

Blanchard, Ken. *The Heart of a Leader.* Colorado Springs, Co.: David C. Cook, 2007.

Brewster, Mike and Frederick Dalzell. *Driving Change: The UPS Approach to Business.* New York: Hyperion, 2007.

Brooks, Arthur C. *Who Really Cares: The Surprising Truth about Compassionate Conservatism.* Cambridge, Mass.: Basic Books, 2006.

Bryson, Kelly. *Don't Be Nice, Be Real: Balancing Compassion for Self with Compassion for Others.* Santa Rosa, Calif.: Author's Publishing Cooperative, 2002.

Collins, Jim. *Good to Great.* New York: HarperCollins, 2001.

Covey, Stephen M.R. *The Speed of Trust: The One Thing That Changes Everything.* New York: Free Press, 2006.

Decker, Bert. *You've Got to Be Believed to Be Heard: Reach the First Brain to Communicate in Business and in Life.* New York: St. Martin's Press USA, 1992.

Dunn, Elizabeth W., Lara B. Aknin, and Michael I. Norton. "Spending Money on Others Promotes Happiness." *Science* 5870 (2008): 1687–88.

Emmons, Robert A. *Thanks!: How the new science of gratitude can make you happier.* New York: Houghton Mifflin Company, 2007.

Ferrazzi, Keith. *Never Eat Alone: And Other Secrets to Success, One Relationship at a Time.* New York: Doubleday, 2005.

Forni, P.M. *Choosing Civility: The Twenty-Five Rules of Considerate Conduct.* New York: St. Martin's Griffin, 2002.

Frankel, Lois. *Nice Girls Don't Get the Corner Office: 101 Unconscious Mistakes Women Make That Sabatoge Their Careers.* New York: Warner Business Books, 2004.

Gladwell, Malcolm. *The Tipping Point: How Little Things Can Make a Big Difference.* New York: Back Bay Books, 2000, 2002.

Goleman, Daniel. *Primal Leadership: Learning to Lead with Emotional Intelligence.* Boston, Mass.: Harvard Business School Press, 2002.

Gonthier, Giovinella. *Rude Awakenings: Overcoming the Civility Crisis in the Workplace.* Chicago: Dearborn Trade Publishing, 2002.

Granovetter, Mark. *Getting a Job: A study of contacts and careers*, 2nd edition. Chicago: The University of Chicago Press, 1995.

Gross, Daniel. *Forbes Greatest Business Stories of All Times*. New York: John Wiley & Sons, Inc., 1996.

Hamlin, Sonya. *How to Talk So People Listen: Connecting in Today's Workplace*. New York: Collins, 2006.

Hornstein, Harvey A. *Cruelty & Kindness: A New Look at Aggression and Altruism*. New Jersey: Prentice-Hall Inc., 1976.

Isen, Alice M. "Positive Affect." In *Handbook of Cognition and Emotion*, eds. Tim Dalgleish and Mick J. Power. Chichester, England: Wiley, 1999.

————. "Success, Failure, Attention, and Reaction to Others: The Warm Glow of Success." *Journal of Personality and Social Psychology* 15, no. 4 (1970).

Josephson, Michael. *The Best is Yet to Come*. Marina Del Ray, Calif.: Josephson Institute of Ethics, 2002.

Kaplan Thaler, Linda, and Robin Koval. *The Power of Nice: How to Conquer the Business World with Kindness*. New York: Doubleday, 2006.

Kearns Goodwin, Doris. *Team of Rivals: The Political Genius of Abraham Lincoln*. New York: Simon & Schuster, 2005.

Laird, James D. "Self-Attribution of Emotion: The Effects of Expressive Behavior on the Quality of Emotional Experience" *Journal of Personality and Social Psychology* 29, no. 4 (1974).

Landry, Craig E. et al., "Toward an Understanding of the Economics of Charity: Evidence from a Field Experiment," *Quarterly Journal of Economics* 121, no. 2 (2006).

Levine, Michael. *Charming Your Way to the Top.* Guilford: The Lyons Press, 2004.

Luks, Allan and Peggy Payne. *The Healing Power of Doing Good: The Health and Spiritual Benefits of Helping Others.* Fawcett Columbine, 1991.

McCarty, Meladee, and Hanoch McCarty. *Acts of Kindness: How to Create a Kindness Revolution.* Deerfield Beach, Fl.: Health Communications Inc, 1994.

McIvor, Olivia McIvor. *The Business of Kindness: Creating Work Environments Where People Thrive.* Lions Bay, B.C.: Fairwinds Press, 2006.

Maxwell, John C. *Ethics 101: What Every Leader Needs to Know.* New York: Time Warner Book Group, 2003.

Michell, Joseph A. *The Starbucks Experience: 5 Principles for Turning Ordinary into Extraordinary.* New York: McGraw-Hill, 2007.

Mitchell, Jack. *Hug Your People: The Proven Way to Hire, Inspire, and Recognize Your Employees and Achieve Remarkable Results.* New York: Hyperion Books, 2008.

Penney, J.C. *Fifty Years with the Golden Rule.* New York: Harper and Brothers, 1950.

Peters, Thomas J. and Robert H. Waterman, Jr. *In Search of Excellence: Lessons from America's Best-Run Companies.* New York: Harper & Row, 1982.

Post, Stephen, and Jill Neimark. *Why Good Things Happen to Good People.* New York: Broadway Books, 2007.

Putnam, Robert D. "E Pluribus Unum: Diversity and Community in the Twenty-first Century. The 2006 Johan Skytte Prize Lecture." *Scandinavian Political Studies* 30, no. 2 (2007).

Robbins, Tony. *Unlimited Power: The New Science of Personal Achievement.* New York: Simon & Schuster, 1986.

Ridley, Matt. *The Origins of Virtue: Human Instincts and the Evolution of Cooperation.* New York: Penguin Books, 1996.

Sanders, Tim. *The Likeability Factor: How to Boost Your L-Factor & Achieve Your Life's Dreams.* New York: Crown Publishers, 2005.

Seligman, Martin E.P. *Learned Optimism: How to Change Your Mind and Your Life.* New York: Pocket Books, 1998.

Shapiro, Ronald M., and Mark A. Jankowski with James Dale. *The Power of Nice: How to Negotiate so Everyone Wins— Especially You!* New York: John Wiley & Sons Inc., 2001 revised edition.

Rath, Tom and Clifton, Donald O. *How Full is Your Bucket?* New York: Gallup Press, 2004.

Truss, Lynne. *Talk to the Hand.* New York: Gotham Books, 2005.

Tuleja, Tad. *Beyond the Bottom Line: How Business Leaders are Turning Principles into Profits.* New York: Facts on File, 1985.

Waldrop, Mitchell M. *Complexity: The Emerging Science at the Edge of Order and Chaos.* New York: Simon & Schuster, 1992.

INDEX

ABOUT THE AUTHOR

Kristin Tillquist's expertise in business spans politics, the law, and internationalism. She is the chief of staff to the mayor of the City of Riverside, the capital city of one of the largest, fastest-growing counties in America. Working with politicians from throughout California and the region, Tillquist knows the techniques of influence that work—and those that don't. A former attorney, she is now a noted business consultant, inspirational speaker, columnist, and teacher/trainer on the value of professionalism and kindness in business.